Paula Deen's

SOUTHERN
BAKING

Paula Deen's

SOUTHERN BAKING

125 FAVORITE RECIPES *from*
MY SAVANNAH KITCHEN

83
PRESS

83 Press
1900 International Park Drive, Suite 50
Birmingham, Alabama 35243
83press.com

ISBN: 978-1-940772-69-1
Printed in China

By Paula Deen

Top row, from left: Bubba Hiers (Paula's brother); Daniel Reed (spouse to Michael's daughter, Michelle); spouses Claudia and Bobby Deen (Paula's younger son). Second row, from left: Ashley Groover (spouse to Michael's son, Anthony); Michelle Reed (Michael's daughter); Corrie Rooks (Bubba's daughter and Paula's niece); Jack (older son of Jamie and Brooke); spouses Brooke and Jamie Deen (Paula's older son). Third row, from left: Anthony Groover (Michael's son); Michael Groover (Paula's husband); Paula Deen; Brian Rooks (spouse to Paula's niece, Corrie). Front row, from left: Henry (older son of Michelle and Daniel); Bennett (son of Anthony and Ashley); Sullivan (son of Corrie and Brian); John (younger son of Michelle and Daniel); Matthew (younger son of Jamie and Brooke).

This book is dedicated to my brother, Bubba, and my Aunt Peggy, the two people who've known me the longest and stood by me through thick and thin.

Contents

Baked with Love

Growing up in Albany, Georgia, I was introduced to good ole Southern cookin' at a young age. I have wonderful memories of being in my Grandmother Paul's kitchen, watching her make yummy peach cobblers, her famous pound cake, fried apple pies, and anything else you could imagine. Grandmother Paul passed on her love of baking to her three daughters, and my mama passed this love on to me. Baked goods have a special place in my heart because they play a role in all our lives and help us celebrate occasions big and small.

Once every few weeks when my brother, Bubba, and I came home from school, there would be a dish of warm and creamy baked banana pudding waiting on us in the kitchen. The aroma would fill the whole house and bring smiles to our faces when it greeted us at the door. We'd grab a spoon and dig into the custardy goodness, chatting about the day between bites. Mama layered her custard with fresh banana slices and just enough vanilla wafers for a subtle crunch and then topped it with a fluffy meringue that she baked until it was lightly, but perfectly, browned. It's impossible for me not to think of my sweet mother when I think of this classic dessert.

I treasure not only the recipes that have been passed down through the generations of my family but also the well-loved cookware that I've inherited, like Mama's tried-and-true cast-iron pans. Daddy would come home every day for lunch, and you could count on Mama being at the stove with something sizzling away in the skillet. I used those same pans to cook and bake for Jamie and Bobby when they were growing up, and I felt like I was honoring Mama. And now that I so enjoy being in the kitchen with my precious grandchildren, I hope that they, too, fall in love with our family traditions just as I did.

This special collection of recipes is packed with Deen family favorites as well as fresh takes on Southern classics. Within these pages, you'll find plenty of versatile bakes that can easily pair with a meal or be eaten alone as a snack. From sunup to sundown, weeknights to special occasions, I've got you covered! You'll find all sorts of cakes, pies, cookies, and bars perfect for a potluck, beloved seasonal flavors for holidays, festive sweets for family celebrations, sweet and savory breads, and delicious dishes to put your trusty skillet to work.

My family is filled with fabulous cooks who have blessed me with great food my entire life, and I want to continue the tradition of passing on recipes and stories to my own family and to y'all. I hope these dishes inspire you to get in the kitchen and spend quality time with loved ones. Southern baking is meant for making memories.

Love and Best Dishes,

CHAPTER 1

Breakfast Treats

I love a hearty breakfast, and Southerners really know what they're doing when it comes to baking up the most important meal of the day. From big ole sweet rolls and muffins to flaky biscuits and bacon-filled scones, these sweet and savory morning-time bakes are worth waking up for and heading to your family table. Share them with your loved ones because the best way to start your day is gathered together.

Coconut Sweet Rolls

These soft spirals combine the best of coconut cake
and sticky buns for a true breakfast indulgence.

Dough:
- 1 (16-ounce) box hot roll mix
- 3 tablespoons granulated sugar
- 1 cup canned coconut milk, warmed (120° to 130°)
- 2 tablespoons unsalted butter, softened
- 1 large egg, room temperature

Filling:
- ½ cup firmly packed light brown sugar
- ¼ cup granulated sugar
- 1 teaspoon ground cinnamon
- ¼ cup unsalted butter, softened
- 1 cup sweetened flaked coconut

Glaze:
- ¼ cup plus 2 teaspoons canned coconut milk
- ½ teaspoon vanilla extract
- 2 cups confectioners' sugar

Garnish: toasted sweetened flaked coconut

1 For dough: In a large bowl, whisk together hot roll mix, included yeast packet, and granulated sugar. Add warm coconut milk, butter, and egg, stirring until combined. Turn out dough onto a lightly floured surface, and knead until smooth, about 1 minute. Cover and let stand for 5 minutes.

2 Spray 2 (8-inch) round cake pans with cooking spray.

3 For filling: In a small bowl, whisk together sugars and cinnamon. On a lightly floured surface, roll dough into an 18x10-inch rectangle. Spread butter onto dough, and sprinkle with sugar mixture and coconut. Starting at one long side, roll up dough into a log, pinching seam to seal. (Trim ends of log, if desired.) Using a serrated knife, cut log crosswise into 12 (1½-inch-thick) slices. Place rolls, cut side up, in prepared pans. Cover and let rise in a warm, draft-free place (75°) until doubled in size, about 1 hour.

4 Preheat oven to 375°.

5 Bake until lightly browned, 20 to 25 minutes, covering with foil halfway through baking to prevent excess browning. Let cool in pans on wire racks for 5 minutes.

6 For glaze: In a small bowl, whisk together coconut milk and vanilla. Gradually add confectioners' sugar, whisking until smooth. Drizzle onto rolls, and garnish with coconut, if desired. Serve warm.

BAKING TIP

Be sure to buy canned coconut milk for this recipe, not coconut milk from the refrigerated dairy section. Give your can of coconut milk a good shake before measuring it.

Chocolate Peanut Butter Banana Coffee Cake

Rise and shine because the early bird gets
the first slice of this decadent breakfast loaf.

Topping:
- 1 cup all-purpose flour
- ½ cup firmly packed light brown sugar
- ½ teaspoon ground cinnamon
- ¼ teaspoon kosher salt
- 6 tablespoons unsalted butter, softened
- ½ cup peanut butter morsels
- ⅓ cup semisweet chocolate morsels
- ⅓ cup chopped roasted salted peanuts

Cake:
- 1 (14-ounce) box banana bread mix
- 1 cup chopped ripe banana (about 2 small bananas)
- 2 large eggs, room temperature
- 1 cup water
- ¼ cup vegetable oil

Glaze:
- ½ cup peanut butter morsels
- 2 teaspoons all-vegetable shortening

1 Preheat oven to 350°. Spray a 9x5-inch loaf pan with baking spray with flour.

2 **For topping:** In a medium bowl, whisk together flour, brown sugar, cinnamon, and salt. Using a fork, stir in butter until crumbly. Stir in peanut butter morsels, chocolate, and peanuts.

3 **For cake:** In a large bowl, toss together bread mix and banana. In a medium bowl, whisk together eggs, 1 cup water, and oil until well combined. Make a well in dry ingredients; gently stir in egg mixture just until combined. Spread batter into prepared pan. Sprinkle topping in large chunks onto batter.

4 Bake until a wooden pick inserted in center comes out clean, 60 to 65 minutes. Let cool in pan for 10 minutes. Remove from pan, and let cool completely on a wire rack.

5 **For glaze:** In a small microwave-safe bowl, heat peanut butter morsels and shortening on high in 15-second intervals, stirring between each, until melted and smooth (about 45 seconds total). Drizzle onto cooled cake.

Apple Cream Cheese Muffins

MAKES 18

The combination of apples and cinnamon is always a fall favorite,
but these indulgent muffins are a hit with my loved ones all year long.

Filling:
- ½ (8-ounce) package cream cheese, softened
- ½ cup granulated sugar
- ¼ teaspoon vanilla extract

Topping:
- ⅓ cup firmly packed light brown sugar
- ¼ cup all-purpose flour
- 1 teaspoon apple pie spice
- 2 tablespoons unsalted butter, softened

Muffins:
- ½ (8-ounce) package cream cheese, softened
- 1½ cups granulated sugar
- ½ cup vegetable oil
- ⅓ cup whole buttermilk
- 2 large eggs, room temperature
- 3 cups all-purpose flour
- 1 tablespoon baking powder
- 1 teaspoon apple pie spice
- 1 teaspoon kosher salt
- 1 cup shredded peeled Granny Smith apple (about 2 medium apples)

1 Preheat oven to 350°. Line 18 muffin cups with paper liners.

2 For filling: In a medium bowl, beat all ingredients with a mixer at medium speed until smooth.

3 For topping: In a small bowl, whisk together brown sugar, flour, and pie spice. Using a fork, stir in butter until mixture is crumbly.

4 For muffins: In a large bowl, beat cream cheese and granulated sugar with a mixer at medium speed until fluffy, 3 to 4 minutes, stopping to scrape sides of bowl. Add oil and buttermilk, beating until smooth. Add eggs, beating until combined.

5 In another large bowl, whisk together flour, baking powder, pie spice, and salt. Add flour mixture to cream cheese mixture, stirring just until combined. Fold in shredded apple. Divide batter among prepared muffin cups. Divide filling among muffin cups, dropping into center of batter. Sprinkle topping onto batter.

6 Bake until golden brown, 25 to 30 minutes. Let cool in pans for 10 minutes; serve warm.

BAKING TIP

After you cube the butter, put it in the
freezer for a few minutes to get it really
cold. Resist the temptation to cut the
butter into pieces that are smaller than
peas; bigger butter pieces mean taller,
flakier biscuits. Use full-fat buttermilk, and
give the container a good shake before
measuring. If the sides of your biscuits are
touching, they will rise higher. Biscuits can
be prepared through step 3 and frozen in
a heavy-duty resealable plastic bag for
up to 2 months. Bake frozen biscuits as
directed for 30 to 35 minutes.

Classic Buttermilk Biscuits

I still vividly remember the soft, fluffy biscuits that my Grandmother Hiers made. They were perfect every single time.

4 cups self-rising flour
2 teaspoons sugar
1 teaspoon kosher salt
1 cup cold unsalted
   butter, cubed
1½ cups cold whole
   buttermilk
2 tablespoons unsalted
   butter, melted
Butter, to serve

1 Preheat oven to 425°. Line a large baking sheet with parchment paper.

2 In a large bowl, whisk together flour, sugar, and salt. Using a fork or pastry blender, cut in cold butter until mixture is crumbly and about the size of peas. Gradually add buttermilk, stirring just until dry ingredients are moistened.

3 Turn out dough onto a lightly floured surface, and gently knead 3 to 4 times. Pat dough to 1-inch thickness. Using a 2½-inch round cutter dipped in flour, cut dough without twisting cutter, flouring cutter between each cut. Gently re-pat scraps and cut to use all dough. Place biscuits on prepared pan, sides touching. Gently press down top of biscuits with your knuckles; brush with melted butter.

4 Bake until golden brown, 20 to 25 minutes. Let cool on pan for 5 minutes; serve immediately with butter.

STEP-BY-STEP

STEP 1 Stop cutting butter into flour when you have pea-size pieces of butter. This helps create tall, flaky layers.

STEP 2 Use a light touch when patting out dough; the more you work the dough, the tougher your biscuits will be.

STEP 3 Flour your cutter between each cut, and make cuts close together to minimize scraps.

STEP 4 Lightly press top of biscuits, and place them on the baking sheet with sides touching so they rise high.

Classic Cinnamon Rolls

MAKES 12

Let the delicious smell of these sweet spirals baking
call your family to the weekend brunch table for you.

Dough:
- ¾ cup whole milk, warmed (105° to 110°)
- 1 (0.25-ounce) package instant yeast
- ½ cup unsalted butter, melted
- ¼ cup sour cream, room temperature
- 2 large eggs, room temperature
- 4½ cups all-purpose flour
- ⅓ cup granulated sugar
- 2 teaspoons kosher salt

Filling:
- ¾ cup firmly packed light brown sugar
- ¼ cup granulated sugar
- 1½ tablespoons ground cinnamon
- ¼ cup unsalted butter, softened
- 1 large egg, lightly beaten

Glaze:
- 1 cup sour cream
- ½ teaspoon vanilla extract
- 4 cups confectioners' sugar

1 For dough: In a medium bowl, stir together warm milk and yeast. Let stand until mixture is foamy, about 10 minutes. Whisk in melted butter, sour cream, and eggs.

2 In the bowl of a stand mixer fitted with the paddle attachment, combine flour, granulated sugar, and salt. With mixer on low speed, gradually add yeast mixture, beating until incorporated, about 1 minute. Switch to the dough hook attachment. Beat at low speed until dough is smooth and elastic, about 5 minutes.

3 Spray a large bowl with cooking spray. Shape dough into a smooth round, and place in bowl, turning to grease top. Loosely cover and let rise in a warm, draft-free place (75°) until doubled in size, 1½ to 2 hours.

4 Line a 13x9-inch baking pan with parchment paper, letting excess extend over sides of pan.

5 Lightly punch down dough. Cover and let stand for 5 minutes. Turn out dough onto a lightly floured surface, and roll into an 18x15-inch rectangle.

6 For filling: In a small bowl, whisk together brown sugar, granulated sugar, and cinnamon. Spread butter onto dough, and sprinkle with sugar mixture, leaving a ½-inch border on one long side. Brush egg wash onto border. Starting at long side of dough with filling, roll up dough into a log, pinching seam to seal. (Trim ends of log, if desired.) Using a serrated knife, cut log crosswise into 12 (1½-inch-thick) slices. Place slices, cut side up, in prepared pan. Cover and let rise in a warm, draft-free place (75°) until puffed and rolls are touching, about 1 hour.

7 Preheat oven to 350°.

8 Bake until golden brown, about 25 minutes. Let cool in pan on a wire rack for 10 minutes.

9 For glaze: In a medium bowl, whisk together sour cream and vanilla. Gradually add confectioners' sugar, whisking until smooth. Spread onto warm rolls. Serve immediately.

Peanut Butter Banana Bread Muffins

MAKES 12

I love the salty, crunchy additions to these otherwise
classic banana bread muffins, and you will, too.

2¼ cups all-purpose flour
1 teaspoon baking powder
1 teaspoon baking soda
½ teaspoon kosher salt
½ cup unsalted butter, melted
½ cup creamy peanut butter
1½ cups mashed ripe banana
(about 4 medium bananas)
1 cup firmly packed light
brown sugar
⅓ cup sour cream
2 large eggs, room temperature
1 teaspoon vanilla extract
½ cup chopped banana
(about 1 small banana)
¼ cup chopped peanuts

1 Preheat oven to 325°. Spray 12 muffin cups with cooking
spray.

2 In a medium bowl, whisk together flour, baking powder,
baking soda, and salt.

3 In a large bowl, whisk together melted butter and peanut
butter. Add mashed banana, brown sugar, sour cream, eggs,
and vanilla, whisking to combine. Fold in flour mixture
just until combined. Fold in chopped banana. Divide batter
among prepared muffin cups. Top with peanuts.

4 Bake until a wooden pick inserted in center comes out
clean, about 25 minutes. Let cool in pan for 10 minutes.
Remove from pan, and let cool completely on a wire rack.

Sticky Monkey Bread

MAKES 8 TO 10 SERVINGS

Ooey-gooey and dripping with richness, this
classic pull-apart bread is beloved for a reason.

1⅓ cups granulated
    sugar, divided
  4 teaspoons apple
    pie spice
  3 (16.3-ounce) cans
    refrigerated honey
    butter biscuits,
    each biscuit halved
  4 tablespoons
    honey, divided
1¼ cups unsalted butter
  ¼ cup firmly packed
    dark brown sugar
  ¼ teaspoon kosher salt

1 Preheat oven to 350°. Spray a 15-cup Bundt pan with baking spray with flour.
In a large resealable plastic bag, combine ⅔ cup granulated sugar and pie
spice, shaking well.

2 Lightly roll each biscuit half into a ball. Add balls in batches to sugar
mixture, and shake to coat. Layer half of biscuit pieces in prepared pan,
and drizzle with 2 tablespoons honey. Top with remaining biscuit pieces,
and drizzle with remaining 2 tablespoons honey.

3 In a small saucepan, cook butter, brown sugar, salt, and remaining ⅔ cup
granulated sugar over medium-high heat, stirring constantly, until sugar is
dissolved. Carefully pour half of sauce onto biscuit pieces; keep remaining
sauce warm over very low heat.

4 Bake until bread is golden brown, 40 to 45 minutes, covering with foil to
prevent excess browning, if necessary. Let cool in pan for 10 minutes. Invert bread
onto a serving plate; drizzle remaining sauce onto bread. Serve immediately.

Glazed Sweet Potato Doughnuts

MAKES 12

Why stand in line for your favorite breakfast treat when you can bake these delicacies at home?

Doughnuts:
- ½ cup unsalted butter, softened
- ½ cup granulated sugar
- ¼ cup firmly packed dark brown sugar
- 2 large eggs, room temperature
- 1 teaspoon vanilla extract
- 2½ cups all-purpose flour
- 2 teaspoons baking powder
- 2 teaspoons pumpkin pie spice
- ½ teaspoon kosher salt
- ⅛ teaspoon baking soda
- ¾ cup mashed cooked sweet potato (about 1 large sweet potato)
- 6 tablespoons whole buttermilk

Glaze:
- 1 cup pure apple cider
- 1¾ cups confectioners' sugar, sifted
- ¼ teaspoon vanilla extract

Garnish: finely chopped toasted pecans

1 Preheat oven to 425°. Spray 2 (6-cup) doughnut pans with cooking spray.

2 For doughnuts: In the bowl of a stand mixer fitted with the paddle attachment, beat butter, granulated sugar, and brown sugar at medium speed until fluffy, 3 to 4 minutes, stopping to scrape sides of bowl. Add eggs, one at a time, beating well after each addition. Beat in vanilla.

3 In a medium bowl, whisk together flour, baking powder, pie spice, salt, and baking soda. In a small bowl, whisk together mashed sweet potato and buttermilk. With mixer on low speed, gradually add flour mixture to butter mixture alternately with sweet potato mixture, beginning and ending with flour mixture, beating just until combined after each addition. Spoon batter into prepared pans. (Cups will be almost full.)

4 Bake until a wooden pick inserted near center comes out clean, about 10 minutes. Let cool in pans for 5 minutes. Remove from pans, and let cool on a wire rack for 5 minutes.

5 For glaze: Meanwhile, in a small saucepan, bring cider to a boil over medium-high heat; cook until reduced to ¼ cup, about 15 minutes. Pour into a small bowl, and let cool to room temperature.

6 Whisk confectioners' sugar and vanilla into reduced cider until smooth. Dip top of warm doughnuts into glaze. Return to rack, and sprinkle with pecans, if desired. Drizzle with any remaining glaze. Let stand for 5 minutes before serving.

BAKING TIP

If you prefer a thicker glaze on your doughnuts, dip them in glaze twice before sprinkling with nuts.

Lemon Poppy Seed Streusel Mini Muffins

Tangy zest and plenty of sweetness will have
you craving these crumbly morning muffins.

Topping:
- ¾ cup all-purpose flour
- ½ cup firmly packed dark brown sugar
- ¼ cup unsalted butter, melted

Muffins:
- 1½ cups all-purpose flour
- ½ cup granulated sugar
- 2½ teaspoons poppy seeds, divided
- 1½ teaspoons baking powder
- ¾ teaspoon kosher salt
- ¼ teaspoon baking soda
- ½ cup whole milk, room temperature
- 6 tablespoons unsalted butter, melted
- 1 large egg, room temperature
- 1 tablespoon lemon zest
- 1½ tablespoons fresh lemon juice
- ¼ teaspoon almond extract

Prepared lemon curd, to serve

1 Preheat oven to 400°. Spray 24 miniature muffin cups with baking spray with flour.

2 **For topping:** In a medium bowl, stir together all ingredients with a fork until crumbly.

3 **For muffins:** In a large bowl, whisk together flour, granulated sugar, 2 teaspoons poppy seeds, baking powder, salt, and baking soda. In a small bowl, whisk together milk, melted butter, egg, lemon zest and juice, and extract. Make a well in center of flour mixture; stir in milk mixture just until moistened. Spoon batter into prepared muffin cups. Sprinkle topping onto batter in large clumps, and sprinkle with remaining ½ teaspoon poppy seeds.

4 Bake until lightly browned and a wooden pick inserted in center comes out clean, 10 to 12 minutes. Let cool in pan for 5 minutes. Remove from pan, and let cool completely on a wire rack. Serve with lemon curd.

Glazed Chocolate Chunk Biscuits

Pair these sweet and decadent breakfast goodies with coffee or milk.

2¾ cups all-purpose flour
2 tablespoons granulated sugar
4 teaspoons baking powder
1⅛ teaspoons kosher salt, divided
½ cup plus 2 tablespoons cold unsalted butter, cubed
¾ cup semisweet chocolate chunks
1 cup plus 1½ tablespoons heavy whipping cream, divided, plus more as needed
1 cup confectioners' sugar
½ teaspoon vanilla extract

1 Preheat oven to 425°.

2 Line a large rimmed baking sheet with parchment paper.

3 In a large bowl, whisk together flour, granulated sugar, baking powder, and 1 teaspoon salt. Using a pastry blender, cut in cold butter until mixture is crumbly. Stir in chocolate chunks. Gradually add 1 cup cream, stirring just until dry ingredients are moistened. (Add more cream, 1 tablespoon at a time, if needed.)

4 Turn out dough onto a lightly floured surface, and gently knead 4 to 5 times. Roll or pat dough to ¾-inch thickness. Using a 2½-inch round cutter dipped in flour, cut dough without twisting cutter, gently rerolling scraps and cutting once. Place 2 inches apart on prepared pan.

5 Bake until lightly browned, 12 to 15 minutes. Let cool on pan for 30 minutes.

6 In a small bowl, whisk together confectioners' sugar, vanilla, remaining 1½ tablespoons cream, and remaining ⅛ teaspoon salt until smooth. Drizzle onto biscuits; let stand until glaze is set, about 20 minutes.

Cinnamon Swirl Coffee Cake

Sweetly spiced and topped with a buttery crumble,
cake for breakfast never tasted so good.

Topping:
- ¾ cup plus 2 tablespoons all-purpose flour
- ½ cup firmly packed dark brown sugar
- 1 teaspoon ground cinnamon
- ¼ teaspoon kosher salt
- 6 tablespoons unsalted butter, melted

Cake:
- 1½ cups unsalted butter, softened
- 1¾ cups firmly packed dark brown sugar, divided
- 1 cup granulated sugar
- 6 large eggs, room temperature
- 1 teaspoon vanilla extract
- 4½ cups all-purpose flour
- 1 tablespoon baking powder
- 1 teaspoon kosher salt
- 1½ cups whole buttermilk, room temperature
- ⅓ cup toasted slivered almonds
- 4 teaspoons ground cinnamon

1 Preheat oven to 325°. Spray a 10-inch tube pan with baking spray with flour.

2 For topping: In a medium bowl, whisk together flour, brown sugar, cinnamon, and salt. Using a fork, stir in butter until large crumbs form.

3 For cake: In a large bowl, beat butter, 1 cup brown sugar, and granulated sugar with a mixer at medium speed until fluffy, 3 to 4 minutes, stopping to scrape sides of bowl. Add eggs, one at a time, beating well after each addition. Beat in vanilla.

4 In another large bowl, whisk together flour, baking powder, and salt. With mixer on low speed, gradually add flour mixture to butter mixture alternately with buttermilk, beginning and ending with flour mixture, beating just until combined after each addition. Spread half of batter into prepared pan.

5 In a small bowl, stir together almonds, cinnamon, and remaining ¾ cup brown sugar. Sprinkle mixture onto batter in pan; top with remaining batter. Using a knife, gently swirl together batter and almond mixture. Sprinkle topping onto batter.

6 Bake until a wooden pick inserted near center comes out clean, about 1 hour and 30 minutes, loosely covering with foil after 30 minutes of baking to prevent excess browning. Let cool in pan for 10 minutes. Remove from pan, and let cool completely on a wire rack.

Vanilla and Lemon Tea Biscuits

MAKES 18

With a hint of citrus flavor, these soft biscuits will melt in your mouth.

2 cups self-rising flour
2 tablespoons
  granulated sugar
½ teaspoon kosher salt
½ cup cold all-vegetable
  shortening, cubed
⅔ cup plus 2 tablespoons
  whole milk, divided
1 (6-inch) vanilla bean,
  split lengthwise, seeds
  scraped and reserved
1½ teaspoons lemon
  zest, divided
1 cup confectioners' sugar

1 Preheat oven to 400°. Line a baking sheet with parchment paper.

2 In a large bowl, whisk together flour, granulated sugar, and salt. Using a pastry blender, cut in cold shortening until mixture is crumbly. Add ⅔ cup milk, vanilla bean seeds, and 1 teaspoon zest, stirring just until dry ingredients are moistened. Turn out dough onto a lightly floured surface, and roll to ½-inch thickness. Using a 2-inch square cutter, cut dough, and place on prepared pan.

3 Bake until bottoms of biscuits are golden brown, 11 to 13 minutes. Let cool slightly on a wire rack.

4 In a small bowl, whisk together confectioners' sugar, remaining 2 tablespoons milk, and remaining ½ teaspoon zest until smooth. Drizzle onto warm biscuits. Serve immediately.

Loaded Banana Bread

MAKES 1 (9X5-INCH) LOAF

My favorite way to mash bananas is in the peel. Gently squeeze whole ripe bananas and then split open the peel. Scrape out the pulp with a rubber spatula or spoon, and it's ready to use.

2 cups all-purpose flour
1 cup sugar
2 teaspoons baking powder
¾ teaspoon kosher salt
¼ teaspoon baking soda
1½ cups mashed ripe banana (about 4 medium bananas)
⅓ cup plain whole Greek yogurt
¼ cup unsalted butter, melted
2 large eggs, room temperature
1 teaspoon vanilla extract
1 cup chopped pecans, divided
½ cup raisins

1 Preheat oven to 350°. Spray a 9x5-inch loaf pan with cooking spray. In a large bowl, whisk together flour, sugar, baking powder, salt, and baking soda. In a medium bowl, whisk together mashed banana, yogurt, melted butter, eggs, and vanilla until smooth. Fold banana mixture into flour mixture just until combined; fold in ½ cup pecans and raisins. Spread batter into prepared pan. Sprinkle with remaining ½ cup pecans.

2 Bake until a wooden pick inserted in center comes out clean, about 50 minutes, covering with foil after 20 minutes to prevent excess browning. Let cool in pan on a wire rack for 10 minutes. Remove from pan, and let cool completely on a wire rack. Store in an airtight container for up to 3 days.

Strawberry Pecan Bread

MAKES 1 (9X5-INCH) LOAF

Berries add a sweet surprise to every bite of this morning delight.

Bread:
- 2 cups self-rising flour
- ¾ cup plus 1 teaspoon granulated sugar, divided
- ½ cup finely chopped pecans
- ¾ cup whole buttermilk
- 2 large eggs, room temperature
- 2 tablespoons unsalted butter, melted
- ½ teaspoon lemon zest
- 1 cup chopped fresh strawberries

Butter:
- ½ cup unsalted butter, softened
- 2 tablespoons confectioners' sugar
- ½ cup coarsely mashed fresh strawberries
- ½ teaspoon lemon zest
- ¼ teaspoon vanilla extract

1 Preheat oven to 350°. Lightly spray a 9x5-inch loaf pan with baking spray with flour.

2 For bread: In a large bowl, whisk together flour, ¾ cup granulated sugar, and pecans. In a small bowl, whisk together buttermilk, eggs, melted butter, and zest. Make a well in center of flour mixture; add buttermilk mixture, stirring just until combined. Gently fold in strawberries. Spread batter into prepared pan.

3 Bake until a wooden pick inserted in center comes out clean, about 45 minutes. Sprinkle hot loaf with remaining 1 teaspoon granulated sugar. Let cool in pan for 10 minutes. Run a knife around edges of pan. Remove from pan, and let cool completely on a wire rack.

4 For butter: In a medium bowl, beat butter and confectioners' sugar with a mixer at medium speed until smooth and creamy. Gradually add strawberries, beating until combined. Beat in zest and vanilla. Serve with bread. Cover and refrigerate remaining butter for up to 1 week. Let cold butter stand at room temperature until softened, about 20 minutes, before serving.

"I always spread a little butter on freshly baked slices of bread and even pound cake. This sweet berry butter is so tasty."—Paula

Cranberry Orange Walnut Muffins

— MAKES 12 —

I packed these yummy muffins with fresh fruity flavor that makes them perfect for a light breakfast or midday snack.

½ cup unsalted butter, softened

¾ cup granulated sugar, divided

¼ cup firmly packed dark brown sugar

2 large eggs, room temperature

1 teaspoon vanilla extract

1 orange, zested

1¾ cups all-purpose flour

1½ teaspoons baking powder

½ teaspoon ground ginger

½ teaspoon kosher salt

½ cup sour cream

3 tablespoons fresh orange juice

1½ cups fresh or thawed frozen cranberries

½ cup finely chopped toasted walnuts

1 Preheat oven to 375°. Spray 12 muffin cups with baking spray with flour.

2 In a large bowl, beat butter, ½ cup granulated sugar, and brown sugar with a mixer at medium speed until fluffy, 3 to 4 minutes, stopping to scrape sides of bowl. Add eggs, one at a time, beating well after each addition. Beat in vanilla and zest.

3 In a medium bowl, whisk together flour, baking powder, ginger, and salt. In a small bowl, whisk together sour cream and orange juice. With mixer on low speed, gradually add flour mixture to butter mixture alternately with sour cream mixture, beginning and ending with flour mixture, beating just until combined after each addition.

4 In a medium bowl, stir together cranberries, walnuts, and remaining ¼ cup granulated sugar; gently fold into batter. Divide batter among prepared muffin cups, filling two-thirds to three-fourths full.

5 Bake until a wooden pick inserted in center comes out clean, about 20 minutes. Let cool in pan for 10 minutes. Remove from pan, and let cool completely on a wire rack. Store in an airtight container for up to 3 days.

Blueberry Muffins with Almond Streusel

MAKES 18

There is nothing like a buttery blueberry
muffin to make busy mornings special.

Topping:
1½ cups all-purpose flour
¾ cup firmly packed light
  brown sugar
½ cup unsalted butter,
  melted
½ teaspoon kosher salt
¾ cup sliced almonds

Muffins:
2½ cups all-purpose flour
1 cup granulated sugar
1 tablespoon baking
  powder
1 teaspoon kosher salt
1 cup plus 2 tablespoons
  whole buttermilk
⅓ cup vegetable oil
2 large eggs, room
  temperature
1 tablespoon orange zest
1¼ cups fresh or thawed
  frozen blueberries
2 tablespoons
  confectioners' sugar

1 Preheat oven to 350°. Line 18 muffin cups with paper liners.

2 **For topping:** In a small bowl, whisk together flour, brown sugar, melted butter, and salt until mixture is crumbly. Stir in almonds. Refrigerate until ready to use.

3 **For muffins:** In a large bowl, whisk together flour, granulated sugar, baking powder, and salt. In a medium bowl, whisk together buttermilk, oil, eggs, and zest. Add milk mixture to flour mixture, stirring just until combined.

4 In a small bowl, gently stir together blueberries and confectioners' sugar; fold blueberries into batter. Divide batter among prepared cups. Sprinkle topping onto batter.

5 Bake until a wooden pick inserted in center comes out clean, 20 to 25 minutes. Let cool in pans for 5 minutes; serve warm.

BAKING TIP

Tossing the blueberries in confectioners' sugar helps keep the color from bleeding through the batter and the blueberries from sinking to the bottom of the cups. If you use thawed frozen blueberries, pat them dry with paper towels before stirring together with confectioners' sugar in step 4.

Strawberry Cream Cheese Danish

Skip the store-bought alternative, and give these homemade pastries a try.

1 (8-ounce) package cream cheese, softened

¾ cup confectioners' sugar, divided

⅛ teaspoon almond extract

½ cup strawberry preserves

1 tablespoon cornstarch

1 (17.3-ounce) box frozen puff pastry, thawed according to package directions

4 tablespoons sliced almonds, divided

2 to 3 teaspoons whole milk

1½ teaspoons unsalted butter, melted and cooled

1 Preheat oven to 400°. Spray 12 muffin cups with baking spray with flour.

2 In a small bowl, stir together cream cheese, ¼ cup confectioners' sugar, and extract until smooth. In another small bowl, stir together preserves and cornstarch until well combined.

3 On a lightly floured surface, unfold one sheet of puff pastry, and gently press just to flatten. Spread half of cream cheese mixture onto dough; spread half of preserves mixture onto cream cheese mixture. Starting at one long side, roll up dough into a log. Cut log into 6 even slices. Place slices, cut side up, in prepared muffin cups. Repeat procedure with remaining pastry, remaining cream cheese mixture, and remaining preserves mixture. Sprinkle 2 tablespoons almonds onto slices.

4 Bake until golden brown, about 25 minutes. Let cool in pan for 10 minutes. Remove from pan, and let cool completely on a wire rack.

5 In a small bowl, whisk together milk, melted butter, and remaining ½ cup confectioners' sugar until smooth; drizzle onto Danish, and sprinkle with remaining 2 tablespoons almonds.

BAKING TIP

Danish can be baked a day ahead, left unglazed, and stored in an airtight container. Loosely cover with foil, and reheat in a 250° oven for 20 to 30 minutes. Drizzle with glaze just before serving. Cover and refrigerate glazed Danish for up to 2 days.

French Toast Casserole

—— MAKES 8 TO 10 SERVINGS ——

Serve an impressive breakfast with ease with this cozy make-ahead casserole.

8 large eggs
1 cup firmly packed light brown sugar
½ cup whole milk
½ cup heavy whipping cream
½ cup maple syrup, plus more for serving
¼ cup unsalted butter, melted
1 tablespoon vanilla extract
2 teaspoons apple pie spice
½ teaspoon kosher salt
1 (16-ounce) loaf challah bread, cut into 1-inch cubes
1 cup dried cherries
½ cup chopped pecans

1 Spray a 13x9-inch baking dish with cooking spray.

2 In a large bowl, whisk together eggs, brown sugar, milk, cream, maple syrup, melted butter, vanilla, pie spice, and salt; stir in bread and cherries. Pour into prepared pan. Cover and refrigerate for at least 8 hours or up to 24 hours.

3 Preheat oven to 350°.

4 Let casserole stand at room temperature for 30 minutes. Uncover and sprinkle with pecans.

5 Bake until golden brown, 45 to 50 minutes. Serve warm with maple syrup.

Cherry Apricot Walnut Bread

MAKES 1 (8½X4½-INCH) LOAF

Dried fruits and crunchy walnuts pair perfectly in this hearty breakfast bread.

¼ cup unsalted butter, softened

1 cup firmly packed dark brown sugar

2 large eggs, room temperature

1 teaspoon vanilla extract

3 cups all-purpose flour

2 teaspoons baking powder

1 teaspoon kosher salt

½ teaspoon baking soda

1 cup whole buttermilk, room temperature

½ cup plus 1 tablespoon chopped toasted walnuts, divided

½ cup dried cherries

½ cup dried apricots, chopped

1 Preheat oven to 375°. Spray an 8½x4½-inch loaf pan with cooking spray; line pan with parchment paper.

2 In a large bowl, beat butter and brown sugar with a mixer at medium speed until fluffy, 3 to 4 minutes, stopping to scrape sides of bowl. Add eggs, one at a time, beating well after each addition. Beat in vanilla.

3 In a medium bowl, whisk together flour, baking powder, salt, and baking soda. With mixer on low speed, gradually add flour mixture to butter mixture alternately with buttermilk, beginning and ending with flour mixture, beating just until combined after each addition. Fold in ½ cup walnuts, cherries, and apricots. Spread batter into prepared pan; sprinkle with remaining 1 tablespoon walnuts.

4 Bake for 20 minutes. Loosely cover with foil, and bake until a wooden pick inserted in center comes out clean, 45 to 55 minutes more. Let cool in pan for 15 minutes. Remove from pan, gently remove parchment, and let cool completely on a wire rack. Store in an airtight container for up to 3 days.

Cinnamon Raisin Swirl Bread

A warm slice of this bread is wonderful with a generous slather of butter, and it makes fabulous French toast.

1¾ cups whole milk, warmed (105° to 110°)

2 (0.25-ounce) packages active dry yeast

6¼ cups all-purpose flour, divided

1½ cups sugar, divided

1½ teaspoons kosher salt

½ cup raisins

¼ cup unsalted butter, melted

3 large eggs, room temperature and divided

2 tablespoons plus 2 teaspoons ground cinnamon

2 tablespoons unsalted butter, softened, plus more for serving

2 teaspoons water

1 In the bowl of a stand mixer fitted with the paddle attachment, combine warm milk and yeast. Let stand until mixture is foamy, about 10 minutes.

2 In a large bowl, whisk together 6 cups flour, ½ cup sugar, and salt. With mixer on low speed, gradually add half of flour mixture to yeast mixture, beating just until combined. Beat in raisins, melted butter, and 2 eggs. Gradually add remaining flour mixture, beating until a soft dough forms.

3 Switch to the dough hook attachment. Beat at medium speed until dough is smooth and elastic, about 4 minutes, adding remaining ¼ cup flour if needed. (Dough should not be sticky.)

4 Spray a large bowl with cooking spray. Place dough in bowl, turning to grease top. Loosely cover and let rise in a warm, draft-free place (75°) until doubled in size, about 1 hour.

5 Spray 2 (9x5-inch) loaf pans with cooking spray. In a small bowl, whisk together cinnamon and remaining 1 cup sugar.

6 Punch down dough. Turn out dough onto a lightly floured surface, and divide in half. Roll half of dough into a 12½x8-inch rectangle. Spread half of softened butter onto dough, and sprinkle with half of cinnamon-sugar mixture. Starting at one short side, tightly roll up dough into a log, pressing edge to seal. Place log, seam side down, in one prepared pan. Repeat procedure with remaining dough, remaining softened butter, and remaining cinnamon-sugar mixture. Loosely cover and let rise in a warm, draft-free place (75°) until doubled in size, about 1 hour.

7 Preheat oven to 350°.

8 In a small bowl, whisk together 2 teaspoons water and remaining egg. Brush egg wash onto dough.

9 Bake until golden brown and an instant-read thermometer inserted in center of loaves registers 190°, 50 to 55 minutes, loosely covering with foil to prevent excess browning, if necessary. Let cool in pans for 10 minutes. Remove from pans, and let cool on a wire rack. Store in an airtight container for up to 3 days.

Sausage, Egg, and Cheese Breakfast Braids

Fuel up for the day with this hearty creation I know your family will love.

¾ **pound ground breakfast sausage**

2 **tablespoons unsalted butter**

8 **large eggs, divided**

1¾ **teaspoons kosher salt, divided**

1 **teaspoon ground black pepper**

¼ **teaspoon dried thyme**

1 **(8-ounce) package shredded sharp Cheddar cheese**

2 **(8-ounce) packages refrigerated crescent dough sheets**

1 **teaspoon sesame seeds**

¼ **teaspoon garlic powder**

¼ **teaspoon onion powder**

¼ **teaspoon poppy seeds**

1 In a large nonstick skillet, cook sausage over medium heat, stirring frequently, until browned and crumbly. Drain well, and transfer to a large bowl. Wipe skillet clean.

2 In same skillet, melt butter over medium heat. In a large bowl, whisk together 7 eggs, 1½ teaspoons salt, pepper, and thyme. Add egg mixture to skillet; cook, stirring frequently, just until eggs are set in large, soft curds. Remove from heat. Gently stir eggs and cheese into sausage.

3 Preheat oven to 400°. Line two large baking sheets with parchment paper.

4 Unroll one sheet of crescent dough onto one prepared pan. Spoon half of egg mixture lengthwise down center of dough, leaving a ½-inch border at each end. Using a sharp knife, cut 1-inch-wide strips along sides of dough. Fold ½-inch borders of dough onto filling; fold side strips of dough onto filling in a crisscross pattern. Repeat procedure on remaining pan with remaining dough and remaining egg mixture.

5 In a small bowl, whisk together sesame seeds, garlic powder, onion powder, poppy seeds, and remaining ¼ teaspoon salt. In another small bowl, whisk remaining egg. Brush egg wash onto braids, and sprinkle with sesame seed mixture.

6 Bake until golden brown, 15 to 20 minutes, rotating pans halfway through baking. Let cool on pan for 10 minutes; serve warm.

BAKING TIP

Braids can be assembled through step 4, covered, and refrigerated overnight.
Brush with egg wash and sprinkle with sesame seed mixture just before baking.

Cheddar, Jalapeño, and Bacon Scones

MAKES 8

These savory scones are a great portable breakfast for any day of the week.

2 cups all-purpose flour

1 tablespoon baking powder

¾ teaspoon kosher salt

¼ teaspoon ground black pepper

¼ teaspoon smoked paprika

6 tablespoons cold unsalted butter, cubed

¾ cup shredded sharp Cheddar cheese, divided

4 slices bacon, cooked and crumbled

1 small jalapeño, seeded and minced

2 tablespoons chopped green onion

1 cup whole buttermilk

1 large egg, room temperature

Garnish: chopped green onion

1 Preheat oven to 425°. Line a baking sheet with parchment paper.

2 In a large bowl, whisk together flour, baking powder, salt, pepper, and paprika. Using a pastry blender, cut in cold butter until mixture is crumbly. Stir in ½ cup cheese, bacon, jalapeño, and green onion. In a small bowl, whisk together buttermilk and egg; add buttermilk mixture to flour mixture, stirring just until combined.

3 Turn out dough onto a heavily floured surface, and knead until dough comes together, 4 to 5 times. Pat or roll dough into a 1-inch-thick circle. Cut into 8 wedges. Place wedges on prepared pan. Sprinkle with remaining ¼ cup cheese.

4 Bake until golden brown and a wooden pick inserted in center comes out clean, about 20 minutes. Garnish with green onion, if desired. Serve warm.

Blueberry Almond Cream Cheese Sweet Rolls

— MAKES 16 —

I like to serve these pillow-soft sweet rolls for a truly decadent start to the day.

Dough:
- 2 cups whole milk, warmed (105° to 110°)
- 2 (0.25-ounce) packages active dry yeast
- 1 cup granulated sugar
- ¾ cup unsalted butter, melted
- 3 large eggs, room temperature
- 1 tablespoon lemon zest
- 1 teaspoon kosher salt
- 8 to 9 cups bread flour

Filling:
- 1 (8-ounce) package cream cheese, softened
- ¼ cup granulated sugar
- 2 cups fresh blueberries
- ½ cup chopped sliced almonds

Glaze:
- 2 cups confectioners' sugar
- 2 teaspoons lemon zest
- 3 tablespoons fresh lemon juice

1 For dough: In a small bowl, stir together warm milk and yeast. Let stand until mixture is foamy, about 10 minutes.

2 In a large bowl, beat granulated sugar, melted butter, eggs, zest, and salt with a mixer at medium-low speed until combined. Add yeast mixture, beating until combined. Gradually add 7 cups flour, beating until smooth. Add enough remaining flour to make a soft dough.

3 Turn out dough onto a lightly floured surface, and knead until smooth and elastic, 6 to 8 minutes. Spray a large bowl with cooking spray. Place dough in bowl, turning to grease top. Cover and let rise in a warm, draft-free place (75°) until doubled in size, about 1 hour.

4 Spray 2 (10-inch) round cake pans with baking spray with flour.

5 For filling: In a small bowl, stir together cream cheese and granulated sugar until well combined. On a lightly floured surface, roll dough into a 24x12-inch rectangle. Spread cream cheese mixture onto dough, leaving a ½-inch border on all sides. Sprinkle blueberries and almonds onto cream cheese mixture. Starting at one long side, tightly roll up dough into a log. Using a serrated knife, cut log crosswise into 16 (1½-inch-thick) slices. Place 8 rolls, cut side up, in each prepared pan. Cover and let rise in a warm, draft-free place (75°) until doubled in size, about 1 hour.

6 Preheat oven to 350°.

7 Bake until golden brown, 35 to 40 minutes. Let cool in pans for 10 minutes.

8 For glaze: In a small bowl, whisk together all ingredients until smooth; drizzle onto rolls. Serve warm.

CHAPTER 2

Cast Iron Comfort

From crispy cornbread and tender scones to fluffy skillet cakes and gooey sweet rolls, recipes baked in cast iron are extra special to my family and me. My collection of tried-and-true skillets of all sizes, wedge pans, and Dutch ovens is so versatile, and I bake with them, just like my mama and grandmama did, for breakfast, lunch, and dinner. No matter which of these recipes you decide to whip up, these delicious cast iron creations will hit the spot every time.

Vidalia Onion Dutch Baby

When I want to put a savory spin on brunch,
this twist on a traditional oven pancake is my go-to.

3 tablespoons vegetable oil, divided

1½ cups sliced Vidalia onions

¾ teaspoon kosher salt, divided

½ teaspoon firmly packed light brown sugar

¼ teaspoon ground black pepper

½ teaspoon fresh thyme leaves

4 large eggs, room temperature

½ cup half-and-half

¾ cup all-purpose flour

1½ teaspoons garlic powder

Garnish: fresh thyme, grated Parmesan cheese, ground black pepper

1 Preheat oven to 450°.

2 In a 12-inch cast-iron skillet, heat 2 tablespoons oil over medium-high heat. Add onion, ½ teaspoon salt, brown sugar, and pepper; cook, stirring occasionally, until onion is translucent, 7 to 10 minutes. Stir in thyme. Remove onion from skillet; wipe skillet clean.

3 Add remaining 1 tablespoon oil to skillet. Place skillet in oven to preheat for 10 minutes.

4 In a large bowl, whisk together eggs and half-and-half until well combined. Add flour, garlic powder, and remaining ¼ teaspoon salt, whisking until smooth. Carefully pour batter into hot skillet, and top with onion.

5 Bake until puffed and golden brown, about 15 minutes. Garnish with thyme, Parmesan, and pepper, if desired. Serve immediately.

BAKING TIP

Don't be alarmed when your Dutch baby starts to deflate as soon as you remove it from the oven; that is exactly what is supposed to happen.

Carrot Cake Wedges

MAKES 8

These wedges make a great snack cake, with or without the frosting.

Cake:
1½ cups all-purpose flour
¾ cup granulated sugar
2 teaspoons baking powder
¾ teaspoon ground cinnamon
½ teaspoon kosher salt
¼ teaspoon ground ginger
2 large eggs, room temperature
¼ cup vegetable oil
¼ cup whole milk
1 (8-ounce) can pineapple tidbits in juice, undrained
1 cup finely shredded carrot

Frosting:
1 (8-ounce) package cream cheese, softened
⅓ cup reserved canned pineapple juice from cake
2 cups confectioners' sugar

Garnish: fresh pineapple

1 Preheat oven to 350°. Lightly spray an 8-well cast-iron wedge pan with baking spray with flour.

2 **For cake:** In a large bowl, whisk together flour, granulated sugar, baking powder, cinnamon, salt, and ginger. In a medium bowl, whisk together eggs, oil, and milk until well combined. Stir egg mixture into flour mixture just until combined.

3 Drain pineapple, reserving juice for frosting. Stir carrot and ⅓ cup pineapple tidbits into flour mixture until combined. (Reserve remaining pineapple tidbits for another use.) Divide batter among prepared wells.

4 Bake until a wooden pick inserted in center comes out clean, 30 to 35 minutes. Let cool in pan on a wire rack for 30 minutes.

5 **For frosting:** In a large bowl, beat cream cheese with a mixer on medium speed until smooth; beat in pineapple juice on low speed until combined. Gradually add confectioners' sugar, beating until smooth. Spread onto cake wedges. Garnish with pineapple, if desired. Serve immediately.

"Pineapple adds fresh, tropical flavor to these little cakes."—Paula

Spiced Bourbon Pecan Bread Pudding

MAKES 6 TO 8 SERVINGS

I filled this decadent treat to the brim with Louisiana-inspired flavors.

1 (16-ounce) loaf brioche bread, cut into 1-inch cubes (about 10 cups)
4½ cups half-and-half, divided
¾ cup unsalted butter
1 cup firmly packed light brown sugar
½ cup granulated sugar
5 large eggs
6 tablespoons bourbon, divided
1½ teaspoons vanilla extract, divided
½ teaspoon ground cinnamon
¾ cup chopped pecans, divided
1 cup confectioners' sugar
¼ cup unsalted butter, melted

1 Preheat oven to 350°.

2 In large bowl, stir together bread cubes and 4 cups half-and-half until coated. Let stand at room temperature.

3 In a 12-inch cast-iron skillet, melt ¾ cup butter over medium heat. Add brown sugar and granulated sugar, whisking until combined. Remove from heat; whisk in eggs, 4 tablespoons bourbon, 1 teaspoon vanilla, and cinnamon until combined. Pour onto bread mixture. Stir in ½ cup pecans. Transfer bread mixture to skillet. Sprinkle with remaining ¼ cup pecans. Cover with foil.

4 Bake for 55 minutes. Uncover and bake until golden brown and a wooden pick inserted in center comes out clean, about 15 minutes more.

5 In a small bowl, whisk together confectioners' sugar, melted butter, remaining 2 tablespoons bourbon, and remaining ½ teaspoon vanilla until smooth; whisk in remaining ½ cup half-and-half until smooth. Drizzle sauce onto warm bread pudding. Serve immediately.

BAKING TIP

Bread pudding can be prepared through step 3 and refrigerated overnight. Let stand at room temperature for 30 minutes while oven preheats; bake as directed.

Blueberry-Lemon Skillet Pound Cake

MAKES 1 (9-INCH) CAKE

Blueberries can be swapped with any other
fresh berry you have on hand in this easy cake.

½ cup unsalted butter,
softened
1½ cups granulated sugar
3 large eggs, room
temperature
1½ teaspoons lemon zest,
divided
½ teaspoon almond extract
1½ cups all-purpose flour
½ teaspoon kosher salt
⅛ teaspoon baking powder
½ cup sour cream
1¼ cups fresh blueberries,
divided
1 cup confectioners' sugar
1½ tablespoons fresh lemon
juice
Garnish: toasted sliced
almonds

1 Preheat oven to 350°. Spray a 9-inch cast-iron skillet with baking spray with flour.

2 In a large bowl, beat butter and granulated sugar with a mixer at medium speed until fluffy, 3 to 4 minutes, stopping to scrape sides of bowl. Add eggs, one at a time, beating well after each addition. Beat in 1 teaspoon zest and extract.

3 In a medium bowl, whisk together flour, salt, and baking powder. With mixer on low speed, gradually add flour mixture to butter mixture alternately with sour cream, beginning and ending with flour mixture, beating just until combined after each addition. Fold in 1 cup blueberries. Spread batter into prepared pan. Sprinkle remaining ¼ cup blueberries onto batter, gently pressing berries into batter.

4 Bake until a wooden pick inserted in center comes out clean, 25 to 30 minutes. Let cool on a wire rack for 30 minutes.

5 In a medium bowl, whisk together confectioners' sugar, lemon juice, and remaining ½ teaspoon zest until smooth. Drizzle onto cake; garnish with almonds, if desired. Serve immediately.

Classic Southern Cornbread

*I always heat my cast-iron skillet in the oven before I pour
in the batter to get a crispy, crunchy crust every time.*

2 tablespoons canola oil
2 cups plain yellow or white
   cornmeal
1 cup all-purpose flour
1 tablespoon baking powder
1½ teaspoons kosher salt
¼ teaspoon baking soda
2½ cups whole buttermilk
6 tablespoons unsalted
   butter, melted
2 large eggs

1 Preheat oven to 425°. Pour oil into a deep 10-inch cast-iron skillet. Place pan in oven until oil is very hot, about 8 minutes.

2 In a large bowl, whisk together cornmeal, flour, baking powder, salt, and baking soda. In a medium bowl, whisk together buttermilk, melted butter, and eggs. Make a well in center of dry ingredients; add buttermilk mixture, stirring until combined. Carefully pour batter into hot oil.

3 Bake until golden brown and a wooden pick inserted in center comes out clean, about 25 to 30 minutes; serve hot.

For an 8-inch skillet:
1 tablespoon canola oil
1 cup plain yellow or white
   cornmeal
½ cup all-purpose flour
1½ teaspoons baking powder
¾ teaspoon kosher salt
⅛ teaspoon baking soda
1¼ cups whole buttermilk
3 tablespoons unsalted
   butter, melted
1 large egg

Prepare batter as directed. Bake until golden brown and a wooden pick inserted in center comes out clean, about 20 to 25 minutes; serve hot.

For a 12-inch skillet:
3 tablespoons canola oil
4 cups plain yellow or white
   cornmeal
2 cups all-purpose flour
2 tablespoons baking powder
1 tablespoon kosher salt
½ teaspoon baking soda
5 cups whole buttermilk
¾ cup unsalted
   butter, melted
4 large eggs

Prepare batter as directed. Bake until golden brown and a wooden pick inserted in center comes out clean, about 30 to 35 minutes; serve hot.

BAKING TIP

The oil should shimmer and start to smoke before the batter is added. This helps the center of the cornbread bake evenly and guarantees a crisp crust. Use a deep skillet so all the batter will fit. To keep the crust crispy, serve the cornbread immediately from the hot skillet. If you prefer to let it cool, turn the cornbread out of the skillet; letting it cool in the skillet will steam the crust.

Vanilla Buttermilk Cake

MAKES 1 (10-INCH) CAKE

A lusciously thick and creamy frosting gives this
simple cake an extra punch of rich vanilla flavor.

Cake:
- ¾ cup unsalted butter, softened
- 1½ cups granulated sugar
- 3 large eggs, room temperature
- 2 teaspoons vanilla extract
- 2 cups all-purpose flour
- 1¾ teaspoons baking powder
- ½ teaspoon kosher salt
- 1 cup whole buttermilk, room temperature

Topping:
- 1 cup fresh blackberries
- 1 cup fresh blueberries
- 1 tablespoon granulated sugar

Frosting:
- 1 cup unsalted butter, softened
- 3 ounces cream cheese, softened
- 1 teaspoon vanilla extract
- 2½ cups confectioners' sugar
- 1 tablespoon whole buttermilk

1 Preheat oven to 350°. Spray a 10-inch cast-iron skillet with baking spray with flour.

2 **For cake:** In a large bowl, beat butter and granulated sugar with a mixer at medium speed until fluffy, 3 to 4 minutes, stopping to scrape sides of bowl. Add eggs, one at a time, beating well after each addition. Beat in vanilla.

3 In a medium bowl, whisk together flour, baking powder, and salt. With mixer on low speed, gradually add flour mixture to butter mixture alternately with buttermilk, beginning and ending with flour mixture, beating just until combined after each addition. Spread batter in prepared skillet.

4 Bake until a wooden pick inserted in center comes out clean, 35 to 40 minutes, loosely covering with foil to prevent excess browning, if necessary. Let cool completely on a wire rack.

5 **For topping:** In a medium bowl, stir together all ingredients; let stand at least 15 minutes.

6 **For frosting:** In a large bowl, beat butter, cream cheese, and vanilla with a mixer at medium speed until creamy. Add confectioners' sugar, beating until combined. Beat in buttermilk until a spreadable consistency is reached. Spread frosting onto cake. Spoon topping onto frosting; serve immediately.

Sweet Orange Marmalade Rolls

MAKES 10

The two toppings spread onto these
citrusy spirals make them doubly delicious.

- 3¼ cups all-purpose flour
- ¼ cup granulated sugar
- 1 (0.25-ounce) package instant yeast
- 1 teaspoon kosher salt
- ¼ cup hot water (120° to 130°)
- ½ cup sour cream, room temperature
- ⅓ cup unsalted butter, melted
- 2 large eggs, room temperature
- 6 tablespoons unsalted butter, softened
- ½ cup plus 2 tablespoons orange marmalade, divided
- ½ cup firmly packed light brown sugar
- 4 tablespoons orange zest, divided
- 2 ounces cream cheese, softened
- 2 tablespoons fresh orange juice
- 2 cups confectioners' sugar

1 In the bowl of a stand mixer fitted with the paddle attachment, combine flour, granulated sugar, yeast, and salt. Add ¼ cup hot water, and beat at low speed until combined. Add sour cream, melted butter, and eggs, and beat just until a soft dough forms. Switch to the dough hook attachment. Beat at low speed for 8 minutes. If necessary, add additional flour, 1 tablespoon at a time, until dough comes together. Cover and let stand for 10 minutes.

2 Spray a 10-inch cast-iron skillet with baking spray with flour.

3 In a small bowl, stir together softened butter and 2 tablespoons marmalade. In another small bowl, stir together brown sugar and 2 tablespoons zest.

4 On a lightly floured surface, roll dough into a 14x10-inch rectangle. Spread butter mixture onto dough; sprinkle brown sugar mixture onto butter, gently pressing into butter. Starting at one long side, roll dough into a log, pinching seam to seal. Using a serrated knife, cut log into 10 slices (about 1½ inches thick), and place cut side up in prepared pan. Cover and let rise in a warm, draft-free place (75°) until doubled in size, about 1 hour.

5 Preheat oven to 350°.

6 Bake for 20 minutes. Cover with foil, and bake until golden brown, 10 to 15 minutes more. Remove rolls from oven, and brush with remaining ½ cup marmalade.

7 In a medium bowl, whisk together cream cheese, orange juice, and remaining 2 tablespoons zest. Gradually add confectioners' sugar, whisking until smooth. Spread onto warm rolls; serve immediately.

Skillet S'mores

MAKES 6 TO 8 SERVINGS

With just three ingredients, this ooey-gooey delight is
the perfect no-fuss dessert to make with my grandbabies.

24 individually wrapped
snack-size milk
chocolate bars,
unwrapped (about
11 ounces total)
2 cups miniature
marshmallows
Graham crackers

1 Preheat broiler. On cooktop, heat a 9-inch cast-iron skillet over high heat until warmed, 2 to 3 minutes. Arrange chocolate bars in skillet, and top with marshmallows.

2 Watching carefully, broil 4 inches from heat until marshmallows are toasted, 1 to 1½ minutes. Serve immediately with graham crackers.

Cheesy Garlic Skillet Rolls

These melty rolls will steal the show at suppertime.

8 low-moisture mozzarella cheese sticks

1 (16-ounce) bag refrigerated deli pizza dough

⅔ cup grated Parmesan cheese

2 tablespoons finely chopped fresh parsley

1 teaspoon garlic powder

1 teaspoon dried Italian seasoning

¼ cup unsalted butter

1 garlic clove, minced

1 Spray a 10-inch cast-iron skillet with cooking spray. Cut mozzarella sticks into 20 (¾-inch-long) pieces; cut remaining mozzarella into small pieces.

2 On a lightly floured surface, roll dough to ½-inch thickness. Using a 2-inch round cutter, cut dough, rerolling scraps to use all dough. Place 1 (¾-inch) piece of mozzarella in center of each round. Wrap dough around cheese, pinching seam to seal.

3 In a small bowl, stir together Parmesan, parsley, garlic powder, and Italian seasoning. In a medium microwave-safe bowl, combine butter and garlic. Microwave on medium in 30-second intervals until butter is melted. Dip each dough piece in garlic butter, and roll in Parmesan mixture to coat. Place dough pieces in prepared skillet, seam side down. Cover and let rise in a warm, draft-free place (75°) until puffed, about 30 minutes.

4 Preheat oven to 400°. Scatter remaining mozzarella pieces on top of dough; sprinkle with any remaining Parmesan mixture. Bake until golden brown, about 15 minutes. Serve immediately.

Berry Cobbler with Cornmeal Biscuits

My grandmother used canned biscuit dough for all her cobblers, but
I put a homemade spin on her classic recipe with these cornmeal biscuits.

1 (16-ounce) container
  fresh strawberries,
  hulled and quartered
2 (6-ounce) containers
  fresh raspberries
2 (6-ounce) containers
  fresh blueberries
1 (6-ounce) container
  fresh blackberries
1 cup plus 1 tablespoon
  granulated sugar, divided
2 tablespoons cornstarch
4 teaspoons orange zest,
  divided
2 tablespoons fresh orange
  juice
1 cup all-purpose flour
1 cup plain yellow
  cornmeal
2 tablespoons baking
  powder
½ teaspoon kosher salt
6 tablespoons cold
  unsalted butter, cubed
⅔ cup plus 2 tablespoons
  cold whole buttermilk,
  divided
Vanilla ice cream, to serve

1 Preheat oven to 375°. Spray a 10-inch cast-iron skillet with cooking spray.

2 In a large bowl, gently stir together all berries, ½ cup granulated sugar, cornstarch, 3 teaspoons orange zest, and orange juice until well combined. Pour mixture into prepared pan. Bake for 20 minutes.

3 Meanwhile, in a large bowl, whisk together flour, cornmeal, ½ cup granulated sugar, baking powder, salt, and remaining 1 teaspoon orange zest. Using a pastry blender, cut in cold butter until mixture is crumbly. Gradually add ⅔ cup buttermilk, stirring until dry ingredients are moistened.

4 Turn out dough onto a lightly floured surface, and gently knead 4 to 6 times. Pat or roll dough to ½-inch thickness. Using a 2½-inch round cutter, cut dough, rerolling scraps once. Transfer biscuits to a baking sheet, and refrigerate while berry mixture bakes. Place biscuits on hot berry mixture; brush with remaining 2 tablespoons buttermilk, and sprinkle with remaining 1 tablespoon granulated sugar.

5 Bake until filling is bubbly and biscuits are golden brown, 15 to 20 minutes more. Let cool for 30 minutes; serve warm with ice cream.

BAKING TIP

Use any single berry or combination of berries
you like; you'll need about 3 pounds total.

Coconut Skillet Cake

Baking this cake in a skillet is a fun and unexpected twist on the classic version.

¾ cup unsalted butter,
  softened
1 cup granulated sugar
4 large egg yolks,
  room temperature
1 teaspoon coconut
  extract, divided
2 cups all-purpose flour
1 teaspoon baking powder
¼ teaspoon baking soda
¼ teaspoon kosher salt
⅔ cup sour cream, room
  temperature
1 cup sweetened flaked
  coconut
1 cup cold heavy whipping
  cream
1 tablespoon
  confectioners' sugar
¼ teaspoon vanilla extract
Garnish: sweetened flaked
  coconut

1 Preheat oven to 375°. Spray a 10-inch cast-iron skillet with cooking spray.

2 In a large bowl, beat butter and granulated sugar with a mixer at medium speed until fluffy, 3 to 4 minutes, stopping to scrape sides of bowl. Add egg yolks, one at a time, beating well after each addition. Beat in ½ teaspoon coconut extract.

3 In a medium bowl, whisk together flour, baking powder, baking soda, and salt. With mixer on low speed, gradually add flour mixture to butter mixture alternately with sour cream, beginning and ending with flour mixture, beating just until combined after each addition. Fold in coconut. Spread batter in prepared pan.

4 Bake until a wooden pick inserted in center comes out clean, 25 to 35 minutes. Let cool completely on a wire rack.

5 In a large bowl, beat cream with a mixer at medium speed until foamy. Add confectioners' sugar, vanilla, and remaining ½ teaspoon coconut extract; beat at medium speed until soft peaks form. Spread whipped cream onto cake; garnish with coconut, if desired.

"My son Jamie just adores coconut cake. This version is easy and fast enough to make any time he has a craving." —Paula

Herb and Roasted Garlic Dutch Oven Bread

— MAKES 1 LOAF —

If you find yeast breads intimidating, this recipe is perfect for practicing. It doesn't require a lot of kneading, and the Dutch oven creates a nice crust.

1 head garlic
½ tablespoon olive oil
1 tablespoon plus ¼ teaspoon kosher salt, divided
4 cups bread flour
1 tablespoon chopped fresh rosemary
2 teaspoons fresh thyme leaves
1 (0.25-ounce) package instant yeast
1⅔ cups warm water (105° to 110°)
Cornmeal, for dusting

1 Preheat oven to 350°. Cut ¼ inch off top end of garlic, keeping cloves intact. Place garlic, cut side up, in a small baking dish. Drizzle with oil, and sprinkle with ¼ teaspoon salt. Wrap garlic in foil. Bake until garlic cloves are soft, about 55 minutes. Let cool completely. Squeeze garlic pulp into a small bowl, discarding skins, and mash with a fork.

2 In the bowl of a stand mixer fitted with the paddle attachment, combine mashed roasted garlic, flour, rosemary, thyme, yeast, and remaining 1 tablespoon salt. Add 1⅔ cups warm water, and beat at medium speed until a wet dough forms, about 30 seconds. Spray a large bowl with cooking spray. Place dough in bowl, turning to grease top. Cover and let rise in a warm, draft-free place (75°) for 2 hours. Refrigerate dough for at least 2 hours or overnight.

3 Turn out dough onto a lightly floured surface, and gently press just to even out dough. Starting on left side of dough and working clockwise, fold edges of dough toward center, pressing gently. Turn dough ball over, and using both hands, cup dough, and pull toward you. Turn dough 90 degrees, and repeat until you have a smooth, tight, sealed round.

4 Line a baking sheet with parchment paper; heavily dust parchment with cornmeal. Place dough round, seam side up, onto parchment. Cover and let rise in a warm, draft-free place (75°) for 1 hour.

5 When dough has 30 minutes left to rise, place empty 6-quart Dutch oven and lid in a cold oven. Preheat oven to 500°.

6 Carefully remove hot Dutch oven from oven. Remove lid, and quickly invert dough, seam side down, into Dutch oven, removing parchment. With a sharp knife, make 2 to 3 shallow cuts crosswise into top of dough (being careful not to touch hot sides of Dutch oven). Cover with lid, and return to oven.

7 Immediately reduce oven temperature to 450°. Bake for 25 minutes. Uncover and bake until an instant-read thermometer inserted in center of loaf registers 190°, about 10 minutes more. Immediately remove loaf from Dutch oven. Let cool on a wire rack for 30 minutes before serving.

Triple Chocolate Brownie Wedges

MAKES 8

Filled, drizzled, and sprinkled with chocolate, these
brownies are a chocolate lover's dream come true.

½ cup unsalted
butter, cubed

8 tablespoons miniature
chocolate morsels,
divided

½ teaspoon vanilla extract

1¼ cups all-purpose flour

⅔ cup granulated sugar

⅔ cup firmly packed
light brown sugar

3 tablespoons unsweetened
cocoa powder

⅛ teaspoon kosher salt

3 large eggs, room
temperature

½ cup white chocolate
morsels

1½ teaspoons all-vegetable
shortening

1 Preheat oven to 350°. Spray an 8-well cast-iron wedge pan
with baking spray with flour.

2 In a medium microwave-safe bowl, microwave butter on
medium, stirring every 30 seconds, until melted (about 2 minutes
total). Stir in 3 tablespoons chocolate morsels until melted and
smooth; stir in vanilla.

3 In a large bowl, whisk together flour, sugars, cocoa, salt, and
3 tablespoons chocolate morsels. Stir in butter mixture until
combined. Add eggs, one at a time, stirring well after each
addition. Spread mixture into prepared wells, smoothing tops.
Gently tap pan on counter twice to release air bubbles.

4 Bake until top of brownies feels dry to the touch and a wooden
pick inserted near outside edge comes out clean, about 25 minutes.
Let cool in pan for 30 minutes. Run the tip of a knife around edges
of brownies; remove from pan. Let cool completely on a wire rack.

5 In a small microwave-safe bowl, microwave white chocolate
morsels and shortening on medium until chocolate is melted
and smooth, stirring every 30 seconds (about 1 minute total).
Drizzle melted white chocolate onto brownies, and sprinkle
with remaining 2 tablespoons chocolate morsels. Let stand until
chocolate is firm, about 30 minutes. Store in an airtight container
for up to 2 days.

Browned Butter, Bacon, and Sage Cornbread

I can't get enough of the savory, nutty flavor that
makes this cast iron cornbread wonderfully unique.

11 tablespoons unsalted butter,
    divided
 2 cups yellow or white
    self-rising cornmeal mix
 1 tablespoon sugar
12 fresh sage leaves, chopped
    (about 1½ tablespoons)
⅓ cup chopped cooked bacon
1½ cups whole buttermilk,
    room temperature
 1 large egg, room temperature
 2 tablespoons honey
Garnish: chopped cooked bacon,
    fresh sage

1 In a medium saucepan, melt 10 tablespoons butter over medium-low heat. Cook, stirring occasionally, until butter turns a medium-brown color and has a nutty aroma, about 10 minutes. Reserve 4 tablespoons browned butter in a small bowl; keep warm for serving. Let remaining browned butter cool to room temperature.

2 Preheat oven to 425°. Place a 10-inch cast-iron skillet in oven to preheat.

3 Meanwhile, in a large bowl, whisk together cornmeal mix, sugar, and sage; stir in bacon. In a medium bowl, whisk together buttermilk, egg, honey, and remaining cooled browned butter. Add buttermilk mixture to cornmeal mixture, stirring just until combined. Carefully remove skillet from oven, and add remaining 1 tablespoon butter, swirling skillet until melted. Pour batter into skillet.

4 Bake until a wooden pick inserted in center comes out clean, 15 to 20 minutes. Serve immediately with reserved warm browned butter. Garnish with bacon and sage, if desired.

Lemon-Lime Buttermilk Scones

These slightly tangy scones are the perfect
accompaniment to a cup of coffee or tea.

Scones:
- 2 cups all-purpose flour
- ¼ cup granulated sugar
- 2 teaspoons baking powder
- 1½ teaspoons kosher salt
- 1 teaspoon lemon zest
- 1 teaspoon lime zest
- ½ teaspoon baking soda
- 6 tablespoons cold unsalted butter, cubed
- 1 cup whole buttermilk
- 1 large egg, room temperature

Glaze:
- 1 cup confectioners' sugar
- 1½ tablespoons whole buttermilk
- ½ teaspoon lemon zest
- ½ teaspoon lime zest
- 1 teaspoon fresh lemon juice
- 1 teaspoon fresh lime juice

Garnish: lemon and lime zest strips

1 Preheat oven to 425°. Spray an 8-well cast-iron wedge pan with baking spray with flour.

2 **For scones:** In a large bowl, whisk together flour, granulated sugar, baking powder, salt, zests, and baking soda. Using a pastry blender, cut in cold butter until mixture is crumbly. In a small bowl, whisk together buttermilk and egg. Add buttermilk mixture to flour mixture, stirring just until combined. (Dough will be wet.)

3 Turn out dough onto a heavily floured surface. Fold dough in half until it comes together, 5 to 6 times. Pat or roll dough into a 1½-inch-thick circle. Cut dough into 8 wedges. Place wedges in prepared wells.

4 Bake until golden brown, about 14 minutes. Let cool in pan on a wire rack for 15 minutes.

5 **For glaze:** In a small bowl, whisk together all ingredients until smooth. Drizzle onto warm scones; garnish with zest, if desired. Serve immediately.

BAKING TIP

If you don't have a cast-iron wedge pan, place the wedges of dough in a 10-inch cast-iron skillet, just barely touching. Bake as directed.

Bananas Foster Upside-Down Cake

This sweet and buttery cake is best enjoyed while it's still warm from the oven.

- ⅓ cup plus ¼ cup unsalted butter, softened and divided
- 1 cup firmly packed dark brown sugar
- 3 tablespoons dark rum, divided
- 2 teaspoons vanilla extract, divided
- 3 firm bananas, halved lengthwise
- ¾ cup granulated sugar
- 2 tablespoons vegetable oil
- 2 large eggs, room temperature
- 2 cups all-purpose flour
- 2 teaspoons baking powder
- ½ teaspoon kosher salt
- ½ teaspoon ground cinnamon
- ¼ teaspoon baking soda
- ¾ cup half-and-half
- ½ cup sour cream
- ½ cup mashed ripe banana (about 1 medium banana)

1 Preheat oven to 350°. Spray a 10-inch cast-iron skillet with baking spray with flour.

2 In prepared skillet, melt ⅓ cup butter over medium heat. Whisk in brown sugar and 2 tablespoons rum; cook, whisking constantly, until sugar is dissolved, about 3 minutes. Remove from heat, and whisk in 1 teaspoon vanilla; let cool completely.

3 Arrange banana slices, cut side down, in sugar mixture in skillet.

4 Meanwhile, in a large bowl, beat granulated sugar, oil, and remaining ¼ cup butter with a mixer at medium speed until fluffy, 3 to 4 minutes, stopping to scrape sides of bowl. Add eggs, one at a time, beating well after each addition.

5 In a medium bowl, whisk together flour, baking powder, salt, cinnamon, and baking soda. In a small bowl, whisk together half-and-half, sour cream, mashed banana, remaining 1 tablespoon rum, and remaining 1 teaspoon vanilla. With mixer on low speed, gradually add flour mixture to butter mixture alternately with half-and-half mixture, beginning and ending with flour mixture, beating just until combined after each addition. Gently spread batter onto banana slices in skillet.

6 Bake until a wooden pick inserted in center comes out clean, 35 to 40 minutes. Let cool on a wire rack for 30 minutes. Run a knife around sides of skillet to loosen cake. Invert cake onto a serving platter; serve warm.

CHAPTER 3

Dinnertime Bakes

At my house, no supper is complete without a bread basket filled to the brim. My memories of stirring together quick breads and rolling out savory biscuits are near and dear to my heart, and this collection contains some of my favorite rolls, muffins, and loaves I've been baking for years. Try your hand at these tasty treats, and your loved ones will come runnin' when the wonderful aromas of these fluffy, freshly baked breads fill your kitchen.

Pepper Bacon Biscuits

The crispy bits of bacon in these flaky, peppered biscuits make for a savory surprise bite after bite.

2 cups all-purpose flour
2 teaspoons baking powder
1¼ teaspoons ground black pepper, divided
½ teaspoon kosher salt
½ teaspoon baking soda
⅓ cup chopped cooked bacon
½ cup cold unsalted butter
1 cup plus 1 tablespoon cold whole buttermilk, divided
2 tablespoons unsalted butter, melted

1 Preheat oven to 425°. Line a baking sheet with parchment paper.

2 In a large bowl, whisk together flour, baking powder, 1 teaspoon pepper, salt, and baking soda; stir in bacon. Grate cold butter into flour mixture; gently stir to coat butter in flour mixture. Refrigerate for 10 minutes.

3 Stir in 1 cup buttermilk just until combined. (Dough will be moist.) Turn out dough onto a lightly floured surface, and gently knead 4 to 5 times. Pat dough to 1-inch thickness. Using a 2½-inch round cutter dipped in flour, cut dough, gently re-patting scraps to use all dough. Place biscuits on prepared pan with sides slightly touching; refrigerate for 10 minutes.

4 Brush with remaining 1 tablespoon buttermilk, and sprinkle with remaining ¼ teaspoon pepper.

5 Bake until golden brown, about 15 minutes. Brush with melted butter; serve warm.

"If you have any biscuits left from supper, split 'em open and tuck a fried egg and cheese inside for the best breakfast sandwich you ever had."—Paula

Cheesy Cornmeal Breadsticks

I like to pair these fluffy breadsticks with soups, stews,
and salads for simple but filling family suppers.

2½ cups warm water
(105° to 110°)
2 (0.25-ounce) packages
active dry yeast
3 tablespoons sugar
½ cup plain yellow
cornmeal
1¼ cups grated Parmesan
cheese, divided
¼ cup olive oil
1 tablespoon plus
⅛ teaspoon kosher salt,
divided
7 to 8 cups bread flour
¾ cup unsalted butter,
softened and divided
1 clove garlic, minced
Garnish: grated Parmesan
cheese

1 In a medium bowl, stir together 2½ cups warm water, yeast, and sugar.
Let stand until mixture is foamy, about 5 minutes.

2 In a large bowl, combine cornmeal, ½ cup cheese, oil, and 1 tablespoon
salt. Add yeast mixture, and beat with a mixer at low speed until smooth.
Gradually add 5 cups flour, beating until smooth. Gradually beat in
enough remaining flour to make a soft dough. Turn out dough onto a
lightly floured surface, and knead until smooth and elastic, 6 to 8 minutes.

3 Spray a large bowl with cooking spray. Place dough in bowl, turning
to grease top. Cover and let rise in a warm, draft-free place (75°) until
doubled in size, about 45 minutes.

4 Line large baking sheets with parchment paper.

5 Turn out dough onto a lightly floured surface, and divide in half.
Roll half of dough into a 12-inch square. Brush with ¼ cup butter, and
sprinkle with half of remaining cheese. Fold dough in half, and roll dough
into a 12-inch square again. Using a pizza cutter, cut dough into 1-inch-
wide strips. Carefully twist dough strips, and place on prepared pans.
Repeat procedure with remaining dough, ¼ cup butter, and remaining
cheese. Cover and let rise in a warm, draft-free place (75°) until doubled
in size, about 45 minutes.

6 Preheat oven to 350°.

7 Bake until golden brown, 15 to 18 minutes. Let cool on pans on wire
racks for 5 minutes.

8 In a small microwave-safe bowl, combine garlic, remaining ¼ cup
butter, and remaining ⅛ teaspoon salt. Microwave on high until butter
is melted. Brush garlic butter onto warm breadsticks, and garnish with
cheese, if desired; serve immediately.

Savory Cheddar Muffins

MAKES 16

These mix-and-pour muffins will disappear in
seconds, so make sure you have plenty to go around.

⅓ cup unsalted butter
¼ cup minced green onion
1 teaspoon minced garlic
1¾ cups whole buttermilk
3 cups Paula Deen Original
Recipes Mix all-purpose
baking mix
1½ cups shredded sharp
Cheddar cheese

1 Preheat oven to 350°. Spray 16 muffin cups with cooking spray.

2 In a small saucepan, melt butter over medium heat. Add green
onion and garlic; cook for 2 minutes. Remove from heat, and let
cool for 10 minutes. Stir in buttermilk.

3 In a medium bowl, combine baking mix and cheese. Add
buttermilk mixture, stirring just until dry ingredients are
moistened. Spoon batter into prepared muffin cups.

4 Bake until golden brown, about 25 minutes. Let cool in pans
for 5 minutes; serve warm.

Cheddar Beer Bread

―――――――― MAKES 1 (9X5-INCH) LOAF ――――――――

This versatile recipe will work with any type of
beer and fresh herb you already have on hand.

3 cups all-purpose flour
2 tablespoons sugar
1 teaspoon baking powder
½ teaspoon kosher salt
½ teaspoon baking soda
1 (12-ounce) bottle lager beer
¼ cup unsalted butter, melted
1 cup shredded extra-sharp
   Cheddar cheese
1 teaspoon chopped fresh dill

1 Preheat oven to 375°. Spray a 9x5-inch loaf pan with cooking
spray.

2 In a large bowl, whisk together flour, sugar, baking powder, salt,
and baking soda. Add beer and melted butter, stirring just until
combined. Fold in cheese. Spread batter into prepared pan, and
sprinkle with dill.

3 Bake until golden brown and a wooden pick inserted in center
comes out clean, 55 minutes to 1 hour. Let cool in pan on a wire
rack for 10 minutes; serve warm.

Garlic Parmesan Spirals

MAKES 24

My love for these bold flavors runs deep, and these simple rolls will be a great addition to your next hearty feast.

1 cup whole milk, warmed (105° to 110°)

5 tablespoons sugar

1 tablespoon active dry yeast

½ cup unsalted butter, softened

1 large egg, room temperature

½ teaspoon kosher salt

3½ cups all-purpose flour

¾ cup grated Parmesan cheese, divided

1½ teaspoons garlic powder

2 tablespoons heavy whipping cream

¼ cup unsalted butter, melted

Garnish: chopped fresh parsley

1 In a small bowl, stir together warm milk, sugar, and yeast. Let stand until mixture is foamy, about 5 minutes.

2 In the bowl of a stand mixer fitted with the dough hook attachment, combine softened butter, egg, and salt. Add yeast mixture, and beat at low speed until smooth. Gradually add flour, ½ cup cheese, and garlic powder, and beat at medium speed until a smooth and elastic dough forms. (Dough will be slightly sticky.)

3 Spray a large bowl with cooking spray. Shape dough into a ball, and place in bowl, turning to grease top. Cover and let rise in a warm, draft-free place (75°) until doubled in size, about 1 hour.

4 Line baking sheets with parchment paper. Divide dough into 24 equal portions. Shape each portion into a 9-inch-long rope. Shape each rope into a spiral, pinching end to seal. Place on prepared pans. Brush tops with cream, and sprinkle with remaining ¼ cup cheese. Cover and let rise in a warm, draft-free place (75°) until doubled in size, 35 to 45 minutes.

5 Preheat oven to 350°.

6 Bake until golden brown, 15 to 20 minutes. Brush with melted butter, and garnish with parsley, if desired. Serve warm.

Sun-Dried Tomato and Basil Quick Bread

This bread is a guaranteed crowd-pleaser—it tastes just like pizza!

3 cups all-purpose flour

2 tablespoons sugar

2½ teaspoons baking powder

½ teaspoon kosher salt

½ cup whole milk

⅓ cup unsalted butter, melted

1 large egg, room temperature

1 cup shredded sharp white Cheddar cheese, divided

5 tablespoons chopped oil-packed sun-dried tomatoes, drained well and divided

4 tablespoons chopped fresh basil, divided

1 Preheat oven to 350°. Spray an 8½x4½-inch loaf pan with cooking spray.

2 In a large bowl, whisk together flour, sugar, baking powder, and salt. In a medium bowl, whisk together milk, melted butter, and egg. Add milk mixture to flour mixture, stirring just until dry ingredients are moistened. Fold in ¾ cup cheese, 4 tablespoons tomatoes, and 3 tablespoons basil. Spread batter into prepared pan, and top with remaining ¼ cup cheese and remaining 1 tablespoon tomatoes.

3 Bake until a wooden pick inserted in center comes out clean, about 35 minutes. Sprinkle with remaining 1 tablespoon basil, and let cool in pan on a wire rack for 10 minutes. Serve warm.

"I love recipes that let the fresh herbs from my garden truly shine."—Paula

Honey Yeast Rolls

I love how the layers of these rolls puff and spread while they bake. They'll really make an impression on your dinner table.

1 cup whole milk

½ cup unsalted butter, cubed

¼ cup honey

4 to 4¼ cups all-purpose flour, divided

2 (0.25-ounce) packages active dry yeast

2½ teaspoons kosher salt

1 large egg, room temperature

3 tablespoons unsalted butter, melted

1 In a small saucepan, cook milk, ½ cup butter, and honey over medium-low heat until butter is melted and mixture registers 120° to 130° on an instant-read thermometer. Remove from heat.

2 In the bowl of a stand mixer fitted with the paddle attachment, stir together 1½ cups flour, yeast, and salt. Add milk mixture to flour mixture, and beat at medium speed for 2 minutes. Add egg; beat at high speed for 2 minutes. Gradually beat in enough of remaining 2¾ cups flour to form a soft dough. Switch to the dough hook attachment. Beat at medium-low speed until a smooth and elastic dough forms, 8 to 10 minutes.

3 Spray a large bowl with cooking spray. Shape dough into a ball, and place in bowl, turning to grease top. Cover and let rise in a warm, draft-free place (75°) until doubled in size, about 45 minutes.

4 Spray 12 muffin cups with cooking spray.

5 Divide dough in half. On a lightly floured surface, roll half of dough into a 14x10-inch rectangle. Cut dough lengthwise into 6 (14-inch-long) strips, each about 1½ inches wide. Lightly brush strips with melted butter. Stack strips, butter side up, on top of each other. Using a sharp knife, cut stack crosswise into 6 (2¼-inch-long) pieces. Place dough stacks in prepared muffin cups, layers facing up. Carefully separate layers to slightly spread apart. Repeat procedure with remaining dough and butter. Cover and let rise in a warm, draft-free place (75°) until doubled in size, about 45 minutes.

6 Preheat oven to 350°.

7 Bake until golden brown, 15 to 18 minutes. Let cool in pans for 5 minutes. Brush with remaining melted butter; serve warm.

Crescent Rolls

———— MAKES 24 ————

Once you've had a bite of these buttery, pillowy rolls,
you'll never reach for the canned version again.

1 cup whole milk
1 cup unsalted butter
¼ cup sugar
¼ cup warm water
   (105° to 110°)
2 (0.25-ounce) packages
   active dry yeast
3 large eggs, room
   temperature
1 tablespoon kosher salt
5 to 6 cups bread flour,
   divided
3 tablespoons unsalted
   butter, melted

1 In a small saucepan, heat milk over medium-low heat just until bubbles form around edges of pan. (Do not boil.) Remove from heat, and add 1 cup butter. Cover and let stand until butter is melted.

2 In a small bowl, stir together sugar, ¼ cup warm water, and yeast. Let stand until mixture is foamy, about 5 minutes.

3 In a large bowl, beat milk mixture, eggs, and salt with a mixer at medium-low speed until combined. Add yeast mixture, beating until combined. Gradually add 4 cups flour, beating until smooth. Beat in enough remaining flour to make a soft dough.

4 Turn out dough onto a lightly floured surface, and knead until smooth and elastic, 6 to 8 minutes. Spray a large bowl with cooking spray. Place dough in bowl, turning to grease top. Cover and let rise in a warm, draft-free place (75°) until doubled in size, about 1 hour.

5 Line 2 large baking sheets with parchment paper.

6 Turn out dough onto a lightly floured surface, and divide in half. Roll each half into a 15-inch circle. Using a sharp knife or pizza cutter, cut each dough circle into 12 wedges. Starting at long end, roll up each wedge, and shape into a crescent, pinching end to seal. Place crescents 2 inches apart on prepared pans. Cover and let rise in a warm, draft-free place (75°) until doubled in size, about 1 hour.

7 Preheat oven to 350°.

8 Bake until lightly browned, 15 to 18 minutes. Let cool on pans for 5 minutes; brush with melted butter. Serve warm.

Spicy Herb Drop Biscuits

MAKES ABOUT 9

When I'm in the mood for a kick of spice, these delicious bites are irresistible.

2 cups all-purpose flour
2 teaspoons baking powder
1 teaspoon kosher salt
1 teaspoon sugar
½ teaspoon garlic powder
⅛ to ¼ teaspoon ground red pepper
1 cup shredded Monterey Jack
   cheese with peppers
2½ tablespoons chopped green onion
1 tablespoon chopped fresh parsley
1 cup whole milk
3 tablespoons unsalted butter, melted

1 Preheat oven to 400°. Line a baking sheet with parchment paper.

2 In a large bowl, whisk together flour, baking powder, salt, sugar, garlic powder, and red pepper; stir in cheese, green onion, and parsley. Stir in milk just until a dough forms. Drop dough by ¼ cupfuls onto prepared pan, spacing about 1 inch apart; brush with melted butter.

3 Bake until golden brown, about 20 minutes; serve warm.

Soda Bread

This hearty bread combines a crusty exterior and soft interior.

1¾ cups all-purpose flour
1¾ cups whole wheat flour
 2 tablespoons sugar
 2 tablespoons
   caraway seeds
 2 teaspoons kosher salt
 1 teaspoon baking soda
 ½ cup cold unsalted
   butter, cubed
1½ cups whole buttermilk
 1 large egg
Prepared herb butter,
   to serve

1 Preheat oven to 375°. Line a large baking sheet with parchment paper.

2 In a large bowl, whisk together flours, sugar, caraway seeds, salt, and baking soda. Using a pastry blender, cut in cold butter until mixture is crumbly. In a small bowl, whisk together buttermilk and egg. Make a well in center of flour mixture; add buttermilk mixture, stirring just until dry ingredients are moistened. (Do not overmix.)

3 Turn out dough onto a lightly floured surface, and shape into an 8-inch circle. Place on prepared pan. Using a sharp knife, cut a cross into top of dough about ½ inch deep.

4 Bake until an instant-read thermometer inserted in center registers 200° and top is golden brown, about 45 minutes. Let cool on a wire rack for 30 minutes; serve warm with herb butter.

Bacon and Cheddar Pull-Apart Bread

I packed this layered bread with enough goodness to make sure there was plenty in every slice.

- ⅔ cup whole milk, warmed (105° to 110°)
- 1 tablespoon sugar
- 1 (0.25-ounce) package active dry yeast
- 3 cups all-purpose flour, divided
- 8 tablespoons unsalted butter, melted and divided
- 2 large eggs, room temperature
- 1 teaspoon kosher salt
- 8 slices thick-cut applewood smoked bacon, cooked and crumbled
- 1 cup shredded sharp Cheddar cheese
- ¼ cup chopped green onion
- Garnish: crumbled cooked bacon, chopped green onion

—— BAKING TIP ——

Add a bit of spice to this crazy-good bread by using peppered bacon and swapping Monterey Jack cheese with peppers for Cheddar.

1 In the bowl of a stand mixer fitted with the paddle attachment, combine warm milk, sugar, and yeast. Let stand until mixture is foamy, about 5 minutes. Add 1 cup flour, and beat at low speed until combined. Add ½ cup flour and 4 tablespoons melted butter, and beat until combined. Add eggs, and beat until combined. Gradually add salt and remaining 1½ cups flour, beating until a soft dough forms. (Dough will be sticky.)

2 Spray a large bowl with cooking spray. Place dough in bowl, turning to grease top. Loosely cover and let rise in a warm, draft-free place (75°) until doubled in size, about 1 hour.

3 Spray a 9x5-inch loaf pan with cooking spray.

4 On a lightly floured surface, roll dough into an 18x16-inch rectangle. Brush dough with 2 tablespoons melted butter, and sprinkle with bacon, cheese, and green onion. Cut dough lengthwise into 4 (18x4-inch) strips. Cut each strip crosswise into 6 (4x3-inch) pieces.

5 Stand prepared pan vertically on one short side, and starting at bottom, carefully layer dough pieces on top of each other in pan. Turn loaf pan upright onto its bottom. Loosely cover, and let rise in a warm, draft-free place (75°) until doubled in size, about 1 hour.

6 Preheat oven to 350°. Drizzle remaining 2 tablespoons melted butter onto loaf.

7 Bake until golden brown, 30 to 35 minutes. Let cool in pan for 20 minutes. Invert onto a serving platter, and garnish with bacon and green onion, if desired. Serve immediately.

Herbed Cloverleaf Rolls

These gorgeous, buttery bakes are so much better than any frozen dinner roll I've ever had and are definitely worth the extra effort.

1 cup whole milk, warmed (105° to 110°)

1 cup whole buttermilk, warmed (105° to 110°)

½ cup plus 2 tablespoons sugar, divided

2 (0.25-ounce) packages active dry yeast

7 cups bread flour

1 tablespoon kosher salt

1 cup vegetable oil

2 large eggs, room temperature, beaten

½ cup unsalted butter, melted

2 tablespoons chopped fresh parsley

2 tablespoons chopped fresh chives

2 tablespoons chopped fresh thyme

1 In a small bowl, stir together warm milk, warm buttermilk, ½ cup sugar, and yeast. Let stand until mixture is foamy, about 5 minutes.

2 In a large bowl, whisk together flour, salt, and remaining 2 tablespoons sugar.

3 In the bowl of a stand mixer fitted with the dough hook attachment, combine yeast mixture, oil, and eggs. With mixer on low speed, gradually add flour mixture, beating until a soft dough forms.

4 Turn out dough onto a lightly floured surface; knead until smooth and elastic, about 5 minutes. Spray a large bowl with cooking spray. Place dough in bowl, turning to grease top. Loosely cover and let rise in a warm, draft-free place (75°) until doubled in size, 1 to 2 hours.

5 Spray 36 muffin cups with baking spray with flour. Punch down dough; cover and let stand for 10 minutes.

6 In a medium bowl, stir together melted butter, parsley, chives, and thyme. Shape dough into 1-inch balls, and dip in butter mixture. Place 3 dough balls in each prepared muffin cup. Cover and let rise in a warm, draft-free place (75°) until doubled in size, 1 to 2 hours.

7 Preheat oven to 350°. Brush dough with any remaining butter mixture.

8 Bake until lightly browned, about 15 minutes. Let cool in pans for 5 minutes; serve warm.

CHAPTER 4

Potluck Perfect

One of my favorite traditions is gathering folks together, with everyone bringing a dish and sharing a meal. And I just love that this tradition is alive and well in the South. I've hosted and attended my fair share of covered-dish dinners, from potlucks and church suppers to family reunions and picnics, and I'm so happy to offer this collection of some of my go-to recipes with y'all. These cookies, cakes, pies, puddings, and more are sure to be a hit.

Peach Pound Cake

This buttery cake is chock-full of one of my favorite fruits—sweet Georgia peaches!

All-vegetable shortening
- 4 cups all-purpose flour
- 3 cups sugar
- 2 cups unsalted butter, softened
- 1 cup whole buttermilk, room temperature
- 6 large eggs, room temperature
- 1 teaspoon vanilla extract
- ½ teaspoon almond extract
- 3½ cups diced peeled fresh peaches, divided
- 1 cup peach preserves, melted

1 Preheat oven to 325°. Lightly grease a 10-inch tube pan with shortening.

2 In a large bowl, beat flour, sugar, butter, buttermilk, eggs, and extracts with a mixer at low speed for 1 minute; scrape sides and bottom of bowl. Increase mixer speed to medium, and beat for 2 minutes; fold in 2½ cups peaches. Spread batter into pan.

3 Bake until a wooden pick inserted near center comes out clean, about 1 hour and 45 minutes. Let cool in pan on a wire rack for 20 minutes. Remove from pan, and let cool completely on wire rack.

4 In a medium bowl, stir together preserves and remaining 1 cup peaches; spoon onto cake just before serving. Refrigerate in an airtight container for up to 2 days.

Mama's Banana Pudding

MAKES 10 TO 12 SERVINGS

My mother made the most wonderful banana pudding
layered with homemade custard and topped with
billowy meringue. This is banana pudding at its best.

Pudding:
1½ cups sugar
¾ cup all-purpose flour
½ teaspoon kosher salt
5¼ cups whole milk, divided
12 large egg yolks
2 tablespoons unsalted
   butter
2 teaspoons vanilla extract
1 (11-ounce) box vanilla
   wafers
4 large bananas, sliced

Topping:
8 large egg whites,
   room temperature
1 teaspoon cream of tartar
1⅓ cups sugar

1 **For pudding:** In a medium bowl, whisk together sugar, flour, and salt; whisk in ¾ cup milk and egg yolks until smooth.

2 In a large saucepan, bring remaining 4½ cups milk to a low boil over medium heat, stirring frequently. Slowly add 1 cup hot milk to egg yolk mixture, whisking constantly. Slowly add egg yolk mixture to remaining hot milk in saucepan, whisking constantly. Bring mixture to a boil over medium heat, whisking constantly. Cook, whisking constantly, until mixture is thickened, about 3 minutes. Remove from heat; whisk in butter and vanilla until butter is melted. Let cool slightly.

3 Preheat oven to 375°.

4 Place one layer of vanilla wafers in bottom of a 13x9-inch baking dish; top with banana slices. Spread pudding onto bananas.

5 **For topping:** In a large bowl, beat egg whites and cream of tartar with a mixer at high speed until soft peaks form. Gradually add sugar, beating until stiff peaks form. Dollop onto pudding, spreading to seal edges.

6 Bake until topping is lightly browned, about 10 minutes. Let cool for 10 minutes; serve warm.

"Have your bowls and spoons ready because I promise you this heavenly pudding will be gobbled up in a flash."—Paula

Lattice-Topped Blackberry Cobbler

A sprinkle of sugar on the lattice crust creates a nice crunch.

2 cups all-purpose flour
¾ cup plus 2 tablespoons sugar, divided
½ teaspoon kosher salt
1 cup cold unsalted butter, cubed
½ cup sour cream
4 tablespoons ice water
10 cups fresh blackberries
5 tablespoons cornstarch
1 tablespoon fresh lemon juice
1 teaspoon lemon zest
1 large egg, lightly beaten
Vanilla ice cream, to serve

1 In a large bowl, whisk together flour, 1 tablespoon sugar, and salt. Using a pastry blender, cut in cold butter until mixture is crumbly. Stir in sour cream. Add ice water, 1 tablespoon at a time, stirring gently just until a dough forms. (Do not overmix.) Turn out dough onto a lightly floured surface, and shape into a disk. Wrap in plastic wrap, and refrigerate for at least 30 minutes.

2 Preheat oven to 400°. Spray a 2-quart baking dish with cooking spray.

3 In a large bowl, stir together blackberries, cornstarch, lemon juice and zest, and ¾ cup sugar. Pour into prepared dish.

4 On a lightly floured surface, roll dough to ¼-inch thickness. Cut dough into 1¼-inch-wide strips. Arrange strips on top of filling in a lattice design. Trim excess dough. Brush dough with egg wash, and sprinkle with remaining 1 tablespoon sugar.

5 Bake for 10 minutes. Reduce oven temperature to 350°, and bake until golden brown and bubbly, about 45 minutes more. Let cool for at least 30 minutes before serving. Serve with ice cream, if desired.

Individual Peach Pies

— MAKES 12 —

These fruity, bite-size pies are perfectly portable for picnics and potlucks.

3 cups all-purpose flour

⅓ cup plus ¼ cup granulated sugar, divided

1 teaspoon kosher salt

1 cup cold unsalted butter, cubed

5 tablespoons ice water

3 tablespoons cornstarch

3 cups chopped peeled fresh peaches

2 tablespoons fresh lemon juice

¼ teaspoon almond extract

Garnish: confectioners' sugar

1 In the work bowl of a food processor, place flour, ¼ cup granulated sugar, and salt; pulse until combined. Add cold butter, and pulse until mixture is crumbly. Add ice water, 1 tablespoon at a time, pulsing 3 times after each addition, just until mixture starts to form a dough. (You may not need the full amount of water.)

2 Turn out dough onto a lightly floured surface, and shape into a disk; wrap in plastic wrap. Refrigerate for 30 minutes.

3 Preheat oven to 375°. Spray 12 muffin cups with baking spray with flour.

4 On a lightly floured surface, divide dough into 3 equal portions. Roll out two portions of dough to ¼-inch thickness. Using a 4-inch round cutter, cut 6 circles from each portion of dough; reserve scraps from each portion of dough. Press dough circles into bottom and up sides of prepared muffins cups.

5 In a medium bowl, whisk together cornstarch and remaining ⅓ cup granulated sugar; stir in peaches, lemon juice, and extract. Spoon peach mixture into dough in cups.

6 On a lightly floured surface, gently pat remaning portion of dough and reserved dough scraps together into a rectangle. Roll dough into a 15x3-inch rectangle. Cut dough lengthwise into 15 (¼-inch-wide) strips. Cut each strip crosswise into 5 (3-inch-long) pieces. Weave 5 dough pieces into a lattice pattern on top of each muffin cup, pressing crusts together to seal.

7 Bake until golden brown, 30 to 35 minutes. Let cool in pan on a wire rack for 15 minutes. Remove from pan, and let cool completely on wire rack. Garnish with confectioners' sugar, if desired.

Heavenly Layered Chocolate Dessert

MAKES 10 TO 12 SERVINGS

Your whole family will rave over this fudgy, indulgent sweet.

1 (15.25-ounce) package chocolate fudge cake mix

½ cup unsalted butter, softened

1 large egg, room temperature

1 (3.9-ounce) package chocolate fudge instant pudding mix

2 cups cold whole milk

1 (8-ounce) package cream cheese, softened

1½ cups confectioners' sugar

1 (16-ounce) container frozen whipped topping, thawed and divided

1 (8-ounce) bag milk chocolate toffee bits

1 Preheat oven to 350°. Spray a 13x9-inch baking dish with cooking spray.

2 In a large bowl, beat cake mix, butter, and egg with a mixer at low speed until well combined. Press mixture into bottom of prepared dish.

3 Bake for 13 minutes. Let cool completely.

4 In a medium bowl, whisk together pudding mix and cold milk for 2 minutes. Cover and refrigerate for 5 minutes.

5 In another medium bowl, beat cream cheese and confectioners' sugar with a mixer at low speed until smooth. Stir in 2 cups whipped topping.

6 Reserve ½ cup toffee bits; sprinkle remaining toffee bits onto cake layer. Spread cream cheese mixture onto toffee bits. Spread pudding onto cream cheese layer. Spread remaining whipped topping onto pudding layer. Sprinkle with reserved toffee bits. Cover and refrigerate for at least 30 minutes before serving or up to 1 day.

7-Layer Bars

MAKES ABOUT 16

I've learned from experience that these decadent bars have
to be made in big batches so that everyone can have a taste.

¾ cup unsalted
butter, softened

1 cup firmly packed
dark brown sugar

1¾ cups all-purpose flour

1¼ teaspoons kosher salt

½ teaspoon baking soda

1 cup old-fashioned oats

½ cup pecans, chopped

1 (12-ounce) package
butterscotch morsels

1 cup bittersweet
chocolate morsels

1 cup sweetened
flaked coconut

½ cup sweetened
condensed milk

1 Preheat oven to 350°. Spray a 13x9-inch baking pan with cooking spray.

2 In a large bowl, beat butter and brown sugar with a mixer at medium speed until fluffy, 3 to 4 minutes, stopping to scrape sides of bowl.

3 In a medium bowl, whisk together flour, salt, and baking soda. With mixer on low speed, gradually add flour mixture to butter mixture, beating to combine. Gradually add oats and pecans, beating just until combined. Using the bottom of a measuring cup, firmly press mixture into bottom of prepared pan. Sprinkle with butterscotch, chocolate, and coconut. Drizzle with condensed milk.

4 Bake until golden brown, 20 to 25 minutes. Let cool completely. Store in an airtight container for up to 3 days.

Spiced Buttermilk Pie

Fragrant spices and tangy buttermilk make
this pie a welcome dessert all year long.

Pie:
- ½ (14.1-ounce) package refrigerated piecrusts
- 1½ cups granulated sugar
- 3 tablespoons all-purpose flour
- ½ teaspoon pumpkin pie spice
- ¼ teaspoon kosher salt
- ¾ cup whole buttermilk, room temperature
- ¼ cup unsalted butter, melted and slightly cooled
- 3 large eggs
- ½ teaspoon vanilla extract

Topping:
- ¾ cup cold heavy whipping cream
- ⅓ cup cold whole buttermilk
- ¼ cup confectioners' sugar
- ½ teaspoon vanilla extract
- ⅛ teaspoon kosher salt

Garnish: ground nutmeg

1 Preheat oven to 425°.

2 **For pie:** On a lightly floured surface, roll piecrust into a 12-inch circle. Transfer to a 9-inch pie plate, pressing into bottom and up sides. Fold edges under, and crimp as desired. Refrigerate for 30 minutes.

3 Top crust with parchment paper, letting ends extend over edges of plate. Add pie weights.

4 Bake on a lower oven rack for 10 minutes. Carefully remove paper and weights. Let cool on a wire rack for 15 minutes. Leave oven on.

5 In a large bowl, whisk together granulated sugar, flour, pie spice, and salt. Whisk in buttermilk, melted butter, eggs, and vanilla until well combined. Pour filling into prepared crust.

6 Bake for 10 minutes. Reduce oven temperature to 350°, and bake until set, 25 to 30 minutes more, covering with foil to prevent excess browning, if necessary. Let cool completely on a wire rack.

7 **For topping:** In a large bowl, beat all ingredients with a mixer at high speed until soft peaks form. Spread onto pie just before serving. Garnish with nutmeg, if desired. Refrigerate in an airtight container for up to 3 days.

Chocolate Pecan Pie Bars

Sweet, crunchy, buttery, nutty—these bars have it all.

4 (5.3-ounce) boxes
shortbread cookies

7 tablespoons unsalted
butter, melted

4 large eggs

1 cup sugar

¾ cup dark corn syrup

2 tablespoons unsalted
butter, softened

2 teaspoons vanilla extract

½ teaspoon kosher salt

2¾ cups pecan halves

1¾ cups semisweet
chocolate chunks

1 Preheat oven to 350°. Line a 13x9-inch baking pan with foil, letting excess extend over sides of pan; spray foil with baking spray with flour.

2 In the work bowl of a food processor, pulse together cookies until ground. Add melted butter, and pulse until well combined. Press mixture into bottom of prepared pan.

3 Bake until crust is just set, about 7 minutes. Let cool completely. Leave oven on.

4 In a large bowl, whisk together eggs, sugar, corn syrup, softened butter, vanilla, and salt. Stir in pecans and chocolate. Pour onto prepared crust.

5 Bake until filling is set, 40 to 45 minutes, loosely covering with foil to prevent excess browning, if necessary. Let cool completely in pan on a wire rack.

6 Using excess foil as handles, remove from pan before cutting into bars. Store in an airtight container for up to 3 days.

BAKING TIP

Let cool completely before cutting into bars so the filling does not run. For clean slices, dip the blade of your knife into hot water and dry it between each cut.

Chocolate Caramel Candy Bar Brownies

Use any candy bar you like, or a mix of several, in these easy bars.

1 (18.4-ounce) box brownie mix
2 large eggs
½ cup vegetable oil
¼ cup water
1 (10-ounce) package shortbread cookies
5 ounces cream cheese, softened
½ cup sugar
1 (11-ounce) package individually wrapped soft caramels, unwrapped
2 tablespoons whole milk
3 (4-ounce) bars semisweet chocolate, chopped
2 tablespoons unsalted butter
1 (8.7-ounce) package Twix Unwrapped Bites candy bars, chopped

1 Preheat oven to 350°. Spray a 13x9-inch baking dish with baking spray with flour. Line dish with parchment paper, letting excess extend over sides of dish.

2 In a large bowl, stir together brownie mix, eggs, oil, and ¼ cup water until well combined. Spread batter into prepared pan.

3 Bake until just set, 15 to 20 minutes. Let cool completely. Position oven rack in top third of oven; leave oven on.

4 In the work bowl of a food processor, place shortbread cookies, cream cheese, and sugar; pulse until well combined. Press mixture on top of cooled brownie layer.

5 Bake for 8 minutes.

6 In a medium saucepan, heat caramels and milk over medium-low heat, stirring frequently, until melted and smooth. Spread onto cookie layer. Freeze until caramel is set, about 30 minutes.

7 In a small saucepan, heat chocolate and butter over low heat, stirring constantly, until melted and smooth. Spread chocolate onto caramel layer; top with chopped Twix bars. Refrigerate until chocolate is set, about 30 minutes. Using excess parchment as handles, remove from pan, and cut into bars.

Strawberry Cream Cheese Snack Cake

MAKES 1 (8-INCH) CAKE

Pack a piece of this subtly sweet cake in
your lunch box for an afternoon treat.

Topping:
- ⅔ cup all-purpose flour
- ⅓ cup firmly packed light brown sugar
- ¼ teaspoon kosher salt
- ¼ cup unsalted butter, melted

Cake:
- ½ cup unsalted butter, softened
- ½ cup plus ⅓ cup granulated sugar, divided
- ¼ cup firmly packed light brown sugar
- 2 large eggs, room temperature
- 1 teaspoon vanilla extract
- 1 teaspoon strawberry extract
- 1½ cups plus 2 tablespoons all-purpose flour, divided
- 1 teaspoon baking powder
- ¼ teaspoon kosher salt
- ¼ cup plus 2 tablespoons whole buttermilk, divided
- 1 (8-ounce) package cream cheese, softened
- ⅓ cup strawberry preserves
- 2 cups thinly sliced fresh strawberries

1 Preheat oven to 350°. Line an 8-inch square baking pan with parchment paper, letting excess extend over sides of pan.

2 **For topping:** In a medium bowl, whisk together flour, brown sugar, and salt. Using a fork, stir in butter until mixture forms large crumbs.

3 **For cake:** In a large bowl, beat butter, ½ cup granulated sugar, and brown sugar with a mixer at medium speed until fluffy, 3 to 4 minutes, stopping to scrape sides of bowl. Add eggs, one at a time, beating well after each addition. Beat in extracts.

4 In a medium bowl, whisk together 1½ cups flour, baking powder, and salt. With mixer on low speed, gradually add flour mixture to butter mixture alternately with ¼ cup buttermilk, beginning and ending with flour mixture, beating just until combined after each addition. Spread batter into prepared pan.

5 In another large bowl, beat cream cheese and remaining ⅓ cup granulated sugar with a mixer at medium speed until creamy, stopping to scrape sides of bowl. Add remaining 2 tablespoons flour and remaining 2 tablespoons buttermilk, beating until combined. Spread cream cheese mixture onto batter. Spread preserves onto cream cheese mixture; top with strawberries. Sprinkle topping in large pieces onto strawberries.

6 Bake until a wooden pick inserted in center comes out clean, 60 to 70 minutes, loosely covering with foil to prevent excess browning, if necessary. Let cool in pan on a wire rack for 15 minutes. Using excess parchment as handles, remove from pan before cutting into squares. Refrigerate in an airtight container for up to 2 days.

Chocolate Cranberry Pecan Oat Cookies

Chocolate, dried fruit, and pecans jazz up standard oatmeal cookies, taking them to the next level.

½ cup plus 3 tablespoons unsalted butter, softened
½ cup granulated sugar
½ cup firmly packed light brown sugar
1 large egg, room temperature
1 teaspoon vanilla extract
1 cup all-purpose flour
½ teaspoon baking soda
½ teaspoon kosher salt
½ teaspoon ground cinnamon
2 cups old-fashioned oats
½ cup semisweet chocolate morsels
½ cup toasted chopped pecans
⅓ cup sweetened dried cranberries

1 Preheat oven to 350°. Line baking sheets with parchment paper.

2 In a large bowl, beat butter and sugars with a mixer at medium speed until fluffy, 3 to 4 minutes, stopping to scrape sides of bowl. Add egg, beating well. Beat in vanilla.

3 In a medium bowl, whisk together flour, baking soda, salt, and cinnamon. With mixer on low speed, gradually add flour mixture to butter mixture, beating just until combined. Stir in oats and all remaining ingredients. Scoop dough by 2 tablespoonfuls, and roll into balls. Place 2 inches apart on prepared pans, and flatten slightly. Freeze for 15 minutes.

4 Bake until golden brown, 12 to 14 minutes. Let cool on pans for 5 minutes. Remove from pans, and let cool completely on wire racks. Store in an airtight container for up to 3 days.

BAKING TIP

Have some fun with flavor variations when making these cookies. Try swapping chocolate, cranberries, and pecans for white chocolate, cherries, and walnuts.

Lemon Bars

MAKES ABOUT 12

Whenever you're craving a refreshing treat,
these luscious goodies will always hit the spot.

2¼ cups all-purpose
 flour, divided
 ¾ cup confectioners'
 sugar
 1 cup cold butter, cubed
 4 large eggs
 2 cups granulated sugar
 2 teaspoons lemon zest
 ½ cup lemon juice
Garnish: confectioners'
 sugar

1 Preheat oven to 350°. Spray a 13x9-inch baking pan with baking spray with flour. Line pan with parchment paper, letting excess extend over sides of pan.

2 In the work bowl of a food processor, pulse together 2 cups flour and confectioners' sugar; pulse until combined. Add cold butter; pulse until mixture is crumbly and just holds together when pressed with fingers. Firmly press mixture into bottom of prepared pan.

3 Bake until edges are golden brown, about 15 minutes.

4 Meanwhile, in a large bowl, whisk together eggs, granulated sugar, lemon zest and juice, and remaining ¼ cup flour until smooth. Pour onto hot crust. (Crust must be hot.)

5 Bake until filling is set, 20 to 25 minutes. Let cool completely in pan on a wire rack. Using excess parchment as handles, remove from pan before cutting into bars. Garnish with confectioners' sugar, if desired.

Coconut Custard Pie

MAKES 1 (9-INCH) DEEP-DISH PIE

This creamy pie has been one of my family's longtime favorites.

1 (14.1-ounce) package refrigerated piecrusts
¾ cup sugar
¼ cup cornstarch
¼ teaspoon kosher salt
6 large egg yolks
1½ cups whole milk
1½ cups canned unsweetened coconut milk
1½ cups sweetened flaked coconut
1½ teaspoons vanilla extract
¼ teaspoon coconut extract
Sweetened whipped cream
Garnish: toasted sweetened flaked coconut

1 On a lightly floured surface, unroll 1 piecrust; lightly brush with water. Stack remaining piecrust on top, and roll crusts to ¼-inch thickness. Transfer crusts to a 9-inch deep-dish pie plate, pressing into bottom and up sides. Trim excess crust; fold edges of crust under, and crimp as desired. Refrigerate for 30 minutes.

2 Preheat oven to 425°. Top crust with parchment paper, letting excess extend over sides; add pie weights. Bake for 15 minutes. Carefully remove pie weights, and bake until crust is golden brown, 10 to 15 minutes more. Let cool completely on a wire rack.

3 In a medium saucepan, whisk together sugar, cornstarch, and salt; whisk in egg yolks until combined. Gradually whisk in milk and coconut milk until smooth. Bring to a boil over medium heat, whisking constantly. Reduce heat to medium-low; cook, whisking constantly, for 5 minutes. Remove from heat; whisk in coconut and extracts. Pour filling into prepared crust. Cover with a piece of plastic wrap, pressing wrap directly onto surface of custard to prevent a skin from forming. Refrigerate until filling is thick and cold before serving, at least 2 hours or overnight.

4 Just before serving, spread whipped cream onto pie, and garnish with coconut, if desired.

Pecan Tassies

I grew up enjoying these traditional Southen bites, and it's so fun to watch my grandbabies fill their little hands with these sweets just like I did.

Crust:
- ½ cup unsalted butter, softened
- 4 ounces cream cheese, softened
- 1 cup all-purpose flour
- ¼ cup plain yellow cornmeal
- ½ teaspoon granulated sugar
- ¼ teaspoon kosher salt

Filling:
- ½ cup firmly packed dark brown sugar
- 1 large egg
- 1 tablespoon unsalted butter, melted
- 1 tablespoon light corn syrup
- 1 teaspoon vanilla extract
- ⅛ teaspoon kosher salt
- ⅔ cup chopped pecans

1 For crust: In a large bowl, beat butter and cream cheese with a mixer at medium speed until smooth. In a medium bowl, whisk together flour, cornmeal, granulated sugar, and salt. With mixer on low speed, gradually add flour mixture, beating until a firm dough forms, stopping to scrape sides of bowl. Shape dough into a disk, and wrap in plastic wrap. Refrigerate for 30 minutes.

2 Preheat oven to 350°. Spray 24 miniature muffin cups with baking spray with flour.

3 Divide dough into 24 equal portions; using lightly floured hands, roll each portion into a ball. Press one dough ball into bottom and up sides of each prepared muffin cup.

4 For filling: In a small bowl, whisk together brown sugar, egg, melted butter, corn syrup, vanilla, and salt until smooth; stir in pecans. Spoon about 1 teaspoon pecan mixture into each pastry shell. (Do not overfill.)

5 Bake until crust is lightly browned and filling is set, about 20 minutes. Let cool in pan on a wire rack for 5 minutes. Run a knife around edges of crusts. Gently remove tassies from muffin cups. Let cool completely on wire rack.

— BAKING TIP —

Baked and cooled tassies can be frozen in a heavy-duty resealable plastic bag for up to 2 months.

Banana Cake with Creamy Frosting

MAKES 1 (13X9-INCH) CAKE

This is Michael's absolute favorite cake. I surprised him with it as his groom's cake at our wedding, so it will always hold a special place in our hearts.

Cake:
- ⅔ cup unsalted butter, softened
- 1 cup granulated sugar
- ½ cup firmly packed dark brown sugar
- 3 large eggs, room temperature
- 1 cup mashed ripe banana (about 2 large bananas)
- 1 teaspoon vanilla extract
- 3 cups all-purpose flour
- 1½ teaspoons baking soda
- ¼ teaspoon kosher salt
- 1½ cups whole buttermilk, room temperature

Frosting:
- ½ cup unsalted butter, softened
- 1 (16-ounce) package confectioners' sugar
- 2 to 4 tablespoons whole buttermilk
- 1 teaspoon vanilla extract
- ½ teaspoon kosher salt

Garnish: sliced bananas, chopped salted cashews

1 Preheat oven to 350°. Spray a 13x9-inch baking pan with baking spray with flour.

2 **For cake:** In a large bowl, beat butter and sugars with a mixer at medium speed until fluffy, 3 to 4 minutes, stopping to scrape sides of bowl. Add eggs, one at a time, beating well after each addition. Beat in mashed banana and vanilla.

3 In a medium bowl, whisk together flour, baking soda, and salt. With mixer on low speed, gradually add flour mixture to butter mixture alternately with buttermilk, beginning and ending with flour mixture, beating just until combined after each addition. Spread batter into prepared pan.

4 Bake until a wooden pick inserted in center comes out clean, 25 to 30 minutes. Let cool completely.

5 **For frosting:** In a large bowl, beat butter with a mixer at medium speed until creamy, 1 to 2 minutes. Gradually add confectioners' sugar, 2 tablespoons buttermilk, vanilla, and salt, beating until smooth. If needed, beat in enough remaining buttermilk until a spreadable consistency is reached. Gently spread frosting onto cooled cake. Garnish with banana and cashews, if desired.

Orange Almond Sheet Cake

Bake this cake with fresh winter citrus, and you'll practically taste the sunshine!

- 1 cup unsalted butter, cubed and divided
- 2 cups granulated sugar
- 1 cup water
- ½ cup vegetable oil
- ½ cup whole buttermilk
- 2 large eggs, room temperature
- 1 tablespoon orange zest
- ½ teaspoon vanilla extract
- ½ teaspoon almond extract, divided
- 2¼ cups all-purpose flour
- 1 teaspoon baking soda
- ½ teaspoon kosher salt, divided
- ⅓ cup whole milk
- 1 (16-ounce) package confectioners' sugar
- Garnish: toasted slivered almonds, orange zest strips

1 Preheat oven to 400°. Spray a 13x9-inch baking pan with baking spray with flour.

2 In a large microwave-safe bowl, heat ½ cup butter on high until just melted, about 1 minute. Add granulated sugar, 1 cup water, oil, buttermilk, eggs, zest, vanilla, and ¼ teaspoon almond extract, and beat with a mixer at medium speed until combined.

3 Sift flour, baking soda, and ¼ teaspoon salt onto butter mixture; beat at low speed just until combined, stopping to scrape sides of bowl. Spread batter into prepared pan.

4 Bake until a wooden pick inserted in center comes out clean, about 20 minutes. Let cool in pan on a wire rack for 30 minutes.

5 In a large microwave-safe bowl, heat milk and remaining ½ cup butter on high until butter is just melted, about 1 minute. Sift confectioners' sugar and remaining ¼ teaspoon salt over milk mixture. Add remaining ¼ teaspoon almond extract, and beat with a mixer at low speed until thick and smooth. Spread frosting onto slightly warm cake. Garnish with almonds and zest strips, if desired. Let cool completely on a wire rack. Store, covered, at room temperature for up to 3 days.

Key Lime Poke Cake

This scrumptious cake is filled with fresh,
Southern flavor straight from the Florida Keys.

Filling:
- ½ cup granulated sugar
- ½ cup fresh Key lime juice
- 3 large eggs, room temperature
- 6 tablespoons unsalted butter, softened
- 2 teaspoons lime zest
- 4 drops liquid green food coloring (optional)

Cake:
- 1 (15.25-ounce) box white cake mix
- ¾ cup water
- ½ cup fresh Key lime juice
- 3 large eggs, room temperature
- ⅓ cup vegetable oil
- 2 teaspoons lime gelatin

Topping:
- 1 (8-ounce) package cream cheese, softened
- 1½ cups cold heavy whipping cream
- 2 teaspoons lime zest
- 1¼ cups confectioners' sugar

Garnish: fresh lime slices

1 **For filling:** In a medium saucepan, whisk together granulated sugar, lime juice, eggs, butter, zest, and food coloring (if using) until well combined. Cook over medium-low heat, whisking constantly, until thickened, 5 to 10 minutes. Strain mixture into a medium bowl; cover with a piece of plastic wrap, pressing wrap directly onto surface to prevent a skin from forming. Refrigerate for 45 minutes.

2 Preheat oven to 350°. Spray a 13x9-inch baking dish with baking spray with flour.

3 **For cake:** In a large bowl, beat cake mix, ¾ cup water, lime juice, eggs, oil, and gelatin with a mixer at medium speed until thick and smooth, 2 to 3 minutes, stopping to scrape sides of bowl. Spread into prepared pan.

4 Bake until a wooden pick inserted in center comes out clean, 25 to 30 minutes. Let cool for 5 minutes. Using the handle of a wooden spoon, poke holes all over top of warm cake. Spread filling onto cake. Let cool completely.

5 **For topping:** In a large bowl, beat cream cheese with a mixer at medium speed until smooth and creamy, about 3 minutes. In another large bowl, beat cold cream and zest with a mixer at medium speed until soft peaks form. Gradually add confectioners' sugar, beating until stiff peaks form. Fold whipped cream into cream cheese until smooth. Spread topping onto cake. Cover and refrigerate for up to 3 days. Garnish with lime slices, if desired.

Pecan Snickerdoodles

Pecans add a nutty twist to these cookie jar classics.

6 tablespoons unsalted butter, softened
6 tablespoons butter-flavored vegetable shortening
1 cup sugar, divided
1 large egg
1 teaspoon vanilla extract
2 cups plus 2 tablespoons all-purpose flour
¾ teaspoon baking powder
¼ teaspoon baking soda
⅛ teaspoon cream of tartar
⅓ cup finely chopped pecans, plus more for sprinkling onto tops
2 teaspoons ground cinnamon
¼ teaspoon ground nutmeg

1 In a large bowl, beat butter, shortening, and ¾ cup sugar with a mixer at medium speed until fluffy, 3 to 4 minutes, stopping to scrape sides of bowl. Add egg and vanilla, beating just until combined.

2 In a medium bowl, whisk together flour, baking powder, baking soda, and cream of tartar. With mixer on low speed, gradually add flour mixture to butter mixture, beating just until combined. Stir in ⅓ cup pecans. Shape dough into a disk, and wrap in plastic wrap. Refrigerate for 1 hour.

3 Preheat oven to 350°. Line 2 baking sheets with parchment paper.

4 In a small bowl, whisk together cinnamon, nutmeg, and remaining ¼ cup sugar. Scoop or shape dough into 1½-inch balls, and generously roll in sugar mixture. Place on prepared pans about 3 inches apart, and gently flatten dough balls to a little more than ½ inch thick. Sprinkle additional pecans on tops, pressing firmly to adhere.

5 Bake until bottoms are golden brown, 10 to 12 minutes. Let cool on pans for 2 minutes. Remove from pans, and let cool completely on wire racks. Store in airtight containers for up to 3 days.

"These cookies are great made with walnuts, too."—Paula

Chess Pie

MAKES 1 (9-INCH) PIE

Chess pie is one of my favorite Southern desserts, and each bite is better than the last.

½ (14.1-ounce) package refrigerated piecrusts
5 large eggs
2 tablespoons water
1 tablespoon lemon zest
½ cup unsalted butter, softened
2 cups granulated sugar
2 tablespoons self-rising flour
2 teaspoons plain yellow cornmeal
Garnish: confectioners' sugar

1 Preheat oven to 325°. On a lightly floured surface, roll dough into a 12-inch circle. Transfer to a 9-inch pie plate, pressing into bottom and up sides. Fold edges under, and crimp as desired.

2 In a medium bowl, whisk together eggs, 2 tablespoons water, and zest until well combined.

3 In a large bowl, beat butter, granulated sugar, flour, and cornmeal with a mixer at low speed until combined. Add egg mixture, beating until well combined. Pour mixture into prepared crust.

4 Bake until center is just set, 40 to 45 minutes. Let cool completely on a wire rack. Garnish with confectioners' sugar, if desired.

Spicy Rosemary Cheese Wafers

MAKES ABOUT 48

No Southern party is complete without cheese straws or wafers. Skip buying preshredded cheese and do it yourself; you'll get much better results.

1 cup unsalted
butter, softened
1 (16-ounce) package
extra-sharp Cheddar
cheese, shredded
2½ cups all-purpose flour
1 tablespoon minced
fresh rosemary
½ teaspoon kosher salt
½ to ¼ teaspoon ground
red pepper

1 Line baking sheets with parchment paper. In the bowl of a stand mixer fitted with the paddle attachment, beat butter at medium speed until creamy. Add cheese, beating until combined.

2 In a medium bowl, whisk together flour, rosemary, salt, and red pepper. With mixer on low speed, gradually add flour mixture to butter mixture, beating until smooth. Using a cookie press or a pastry bag fitted with a large, flat, wavy tip, pipe mixture to desired lengths on prepared pans, cutting ends with a knife. Freeze for at least 1 hour.

3 Preheat oven to 300°. Bake until bottoms of straws are lightly browned, about 20 minutes. Let cool on pans for 5 minutes. Remove from pans, and let cool completely on wire racks. Store in an airtight container for up to 1 week.

Cold-Oven Pound Cake

───── MAKES 1 (10-INCH) CAKE ─────

Starting with a cold oven lets this cake bake slowly, giving it a crunchy top and soft interior that you just can't get any other way.

1 cup unsalted butter, softened
3 cups sugar
6 large eggs, room temperature
2 teaspoons vanilla extract
3 cups all-purpose flour
¾ teaspoon kosher salt
¾ cup heavy whipping cream, room temperature

1 Spray a 10-inch tube pan with baking spray with flour.

2 In the bowl of a stand mixer fitted with the paddle attachment, beat butter and sugar at high speed until fluffy, 2 to 3 minutes, stopping to scrape sides of bowl. Add eggs, one at a time, beating well after each addition. Beat in vanilla.

3 In a medium bowl, whisk together flour and salt. With mixer on low speed, gradually add flour mixture to butter mixture alternately with cream, beginning and ending with flour mixture, beating just until combined after each addition. Spread batter into prepared pan. Gently tap pan on counter twice to release air bubbles.

4 Place pan in a cold oven, and bake at 325° until a wooden pick inserted near center comes out with a few moist crumbs attached, about 75 minutes. Let cool in pan for 30 minutes. Remove from pan, and let cool completely, top side up, on a wire rack. Store in an airtight container for up to 3 days.

───── BAKING TIP ─────

Be sure your butter isn't too soft; it should hold an indentation when pressed with your finger, but your finger should not go all the way through the butter. For best results, use a light-colored tube pan that does not have a removable bottom. If you have a dark tube pan, wrap the bottom and sides of the pan in foil to help prevent the cake from overbrowning.

Triple-Chocolate Oat Cake

MAKES 1 (13X9-INCH) CAKE

Nothing soothes my soul quite like chocolate,
and this decadent cake will melt in your mouth.

Cake:
1¾ cups boiling water
1 cup old-fashioned oats
½ cup unsalted
   butter, melted
1 cup granulated sugar
1 cup firmly packed dark
   brown sugar
1 teaspoon vanilla extract
3 large eggs, room
   temperature
1¾ cups all-purpose flour
2 tablespoons unsweetened
   cocoa powder
1 teaspoon baking soda
½ teaspoon kosher salt
½ teaspoon ground
   cinnamon
1⅓ cups semisweet
   chocolate morsels

Frosting:
½ cup unsweetened
   cocoa powder
½ cup unsalted butter
½ cup heavy whipping cream
1 tablespoon unsulphured
   molasses
3 cups confectioners'
   sugar, sifted
1 teaspoon vanilla extract

Garnish: chopped walnuts

1 Preheat oven to 350°. Spray a 13x9-inch baking pan with baking spray with flour.

2 **For cake:** In a small bowl, stir together 1¾ cups boiling water and oats; let stand for 10 minutes.

3 In a large bowl, beat melted butter and sugars with a mixer at medium speed until well combined. Beat in vanilla. Add eggs, one at a time, beating well after each addition.

4 In a medium bowl, whisk together flour, cocoa, baking soda, salt, and cinnamon. With mixer on low speed, gradually add flour mixture to butter mixture, beating just until combined. Stir in oats and chocolate morsels until well combined. Pour batter into prepared pan.

5 Bake until a wooden pick inserted in center comes out clean, about 25 minutes.

6 **For frosting:** In a medium saucepan, cook cocoa, butter, cream, and molasses over medium heat, whisking occasionally, until melted and smooth. Remove from heat; whisk in confectioners' sugar, 1 cup at a time. Whisk in vanilla. Spread warm frosting onto warm cake. Garnish with walnuts, if desired. Let cool completely in pan on a wire rack. Cover and store for up to 3 days.

Frosted Orange Blondies

The team at my magazine, *Cooking with Paula Deen*, based this recipe on a citrus brownie that I've been making for years. They took a pretty good thing and made it even better!

Blondies:

- 1 cup unsalted butter, softened
- 2½ cups granulated sugar
- 3 large eggs
- 2 teaspoons orange zest
- 1 teaspoon orange extract
- 1 teaspoon vanilla extract
- 3 cups all-purpose flour
- ½ teaspoon baking powder
- ⅛ teaspoon kosher salt

Frosting:

- 1 (8-ounce) package cream cheese, softened
- ½ cup unsalted butter, softened
- 1 tablespoon orange zest
- 2 cups confectioners' sugar

Garnish: orange zest

1 Preheat oven to 350°. Spray a 13x9-inch baking pan with cooking spray. Line pan with parchment paper, letting excess extend over sides of pan.

2 **For blondies:** In a large bowl, beat butter and granulated sugar with a mixer at medium speed until fluffy, 3 to 4 minutes, stopping to scrape sides of bowl. Add eggs, one at a time, beating well after each addition. Beat in zest and extracts.

3 In a medium bowl, whisk together flour, baking powder, and salt. With mixer on low speed, gradually add flour mixture to butter mixture, beating just until combined. Spread batter into prepared pan.

4 Bake until a wooden pick inserted in center comes out clean, about 25 minutes. Let cool completely in pan on a wire rack.

5 **For frosting:** In a large bowl, beat cream cheese and butter with a mixer at medium speed until smooth; beat in zest. With mixer on low speed, gradually add confectioners' sugar, beating until smooth.

6 Using excess parchment as handles, remove blondies from pan, and spread frosting onto blondies. Garnish with zest, if desired. Cut into bars. Cover and refrigerate for up to 3 days.

Salted Caramel Sheet Cake

MAKES 1 (13X9-INCH) CAKE

My son Bobby's favorite dessert is caramel cake. It's always worth the effort to make, but this sheet cake version makes it an easy treat.

Cake:
- 1 cup unsalted butter, softened
- 1½ cups granulated sugar
- 4 large eggs, room temperature, separated
- 1 teaspoon vanilla extract
- 3 cups cake flour
- 1 teaspoon baking powder
- 1 teaspoon baking soda
- ½ teaspoon kosher salt
- 1¼ cups whole buttermilk, room temperature

Frosting:
- 3 cups confectioners' sugar
- ¾ cup unsalted butter
- 1½ cups firmly packed dark brown sugar
- 5 tablespoons whole buttermilk
- 1½ teaspoons vanilla extract

Garnish: chopped toasted pecans, flaked sea salt

1 Preheat oven to 350°. Spray a 13x9-inch baking dish with baking spray with flour.

2 **For cake:** In a large bowl, beat butter and granulated sugar with a mixer at medium speed until fluffy, 3 to 4 minutes, stopping to scrape sides of bowl. Add egg yolks, one at a time, beating well after each addition. Beat in vanilla.

3 In a medium bowl, whisk together flour, baking powder, baking soda, and salt. With mixer on low speed, gradually add flour mixture to butter mixture alternately with buttermilk, beginning and ending with flour mixture, beating just until combined after each addition.

4 In another medium bowl, using clean beaters, beat egg whites with a mixer at high speed just until stiff peaks form. (Do not overbeat.) Gently fold egg whites into batter. Spread batter into prepared pan.

5 Bake until a wooden pick inserted in center comes out clean, 25 to 30 minutes. Let cool completely on a wire rack.

6 **For frosting:** Sift confectioners' sugar into a large bowl. In a medium heavy-bottomed saucepan, melt butter over medium heat. Stir in brown sugar; cook for 1 minute, stirring constantly. Remove from heat; stir in buttermilk. Return to heat; bring mixture to a low boil, and cook for 1 minute, stirring constantly.

7 Add brown sugar mixture and vanilla to confectioners' sugar, and beat with a mixer at medium speed until smooth. Pour frosting onto cake, and spread with an offset spatula until frosting begins to thicken. Garnish with pecans and sea salt, if desired. Store, covered, at room temperature for up to 3 days.

Strawberry Sheet Cake

MAKES 1 (13X9-INCH) CAKE

It's hard to beat bright summer strawberries, and piling them
onto this cake makes a simple but oh-so-pretty garnish!

Cake:
- 1 cup unsalted butter, softened
- 1⅔ cups granulated sugar
- 1 (3-ounce) box strawberry gelatin
- 3 large eggs, room temperature
- 2½ cups all-purpose flour
- ½ teaspoon baking powder
- ½ teaspoon baking soda
- ¼ teaspoon kosher salt
- 1 cup whole buttermilk, room temperature
- ½ cup finely chopped fresh strawberries

Frosting:
- 1 (8-ounce) package cream cheese, softened
- ¼ cup unsalted butter, softened
- ½ cup finely chopped fresh strawberries
- ½ teaspoon vanilla extract
- Pinch kosher salt
- 6 cups confectioners' sugar

Garnish: fresh strawberries

1 Preheat oven to 325°. Spray a 13x9-inch baking pan with baking spray with flour.

2 **For cake:** In a large bowl, beat butter, granulated sugar, and gelatin with a mixer at medium speed until fluffy, 3 to 4 minutes, stopping to scrape sides of bowl. Add eggs, one at a time, beating well after each addition.

3 In a medium bowl, whisk together flour, baking powder, baking soda, and salt. With mixer on low speed, gradually add flour mixture to butter mixture alternately with buttermilk, beginning and ending with flour mixture, beating just until combined after each addition. Stir in strawberries. Spread batter into prepared pan.

4 Bake until a wooden pick inserted in center comes out clean, 35 to 45 minutes. Let cool completely on a wire rack.

5 **For frosting:** In a large bowl, beat cream cheese and butter with a mixer at medium speed until smooth. Add strawberries, vanilla, and salt, beating until combined. Gradually add confectioners' sugar, beating until smooth. Spread frosting onto cooled cake. Garnish with strawberries, if desired. Cover and refrigerate for up to 3 days.

Plum, Peach, and Nectarine Crisp

MAKES 6 TO 8 SERVINGS

When juicy stone fruits are in peak season, gather
them up to use in this easy mix-and-stir dessert.

3 cups sliced fresh plums
2 cups sliced peeled fresh peaches
2 cups sliced fresh nectarines
½ cup granulated sugar
½ cup plus 3 tablespoons
   all-purpose flour, divided
¼ teaspoon orange zest
1 tablespoon fresh orange juice
½ cup old-fashioned oats
½ cup firmly packed light
   brown sugar
½ cup unsalted butter, softened
⅓ cup chopped pecans
½ teaspoon kosher salt
¼ teaspoon baking powder
¼ teaspoon ground cinnamon

1 Preheat oven to 350°.

2 In a large bowl, stir together plums, peaches, nectarines, granulated sugar, 3 tablespoons flour, and orange zest and juice. Pour mixture into a 2-quart baking dish.

3 In same bowl, stir together oats, brown sugar, butter, pecans, salt, baking powder, cinnamon, and remaining ½ cup flour until well combined. Sprinkle mixture onto fruit.

4 Bake until golden brown and bubbly, 30 to 40 minutes. Let cool for at least 30 minutes before serving.

Root Beer Bundt Cake

MAKES 1 (12-CUP) BUNDT CAKE

I like to use Southern brands of root beer such as Abita and Barq's in this cake. They have a nice strong flavor that comes through.

1 (16.25-ounce) box vanilla cake mix
1¼ cups root beer (not diet), room temperature
⅓ cup vegetable oil
3 large egg whites
1 teaspoon root beer extract
Garnish: confectioners' sugar

1 Preheat oven to 350°. Spray a 12-cup Bundt pan with baking spray with flour.

2 In a large bowl, beat cake mix, root beer, oil, egg whites, and extract with a mixer at low speed until combined, about 30 seconds. Increase mixer speed to medium, and beat for 2 minutes, stopping to scrape sides of bowl. Spoon batter into prepared pan. Gently tap pan on counter twice.

3 Bake until a wooden pick inserted near center comes out clean, about 35 minutes. Let cool in pan for 10 minutes. Remove from pan, and let cool completely on a wire rack. Garnish with confectioners' sugar, if desired. Store in an airtight container for up to 3 days.

Peanut Butter Cupcakes

I can't leave these goodies on the counter for more than five minutes before one mysteriously disappears. They're always a huge hit!

Cupcakes:
- 1 (15.25-ounce) box white cake mix
- 1 cup whole milk
- ½ cup unsalted butter, melted
- ½ cup creamy peanut butter
- 3 large eggs, room temperature

Frosting:
- ½ cup unsalted butter, softened
- ½ cup creamy peanut butter
- 1 (2-pound) package confectioners' sugar
- 3 tablespoons whole milk

Garnish: chopped salted peanuts, miniature peanut butter cups

1 Preheat oven to 350°. Line 24 muffin cups with paper liners.

2 **For cupcakes:** In a large bowl, beat all ingredients with a mixer at medium speed until thick and smooth, about 2 minutes. Spoon batter into prepared muffin cups.

3 Bake until a wooden pick inserted in center comes out clean, 18 to 20 minutes. Let cool in pans for 10 minutes. Remove from pans, and let cool completely on wire racks.

4 **For frosting:** In a large bowl, beat butter and peanut butter with a mixer at medium speed until smooth, stopping to scrape sides of bowl. Gradually add confectioners' sugar and milk, beating until smooth. Spread or pipe frosting onto cooled cupcakes. Garnish with peanuts and peanut butter cups, if desired. Store in an airtight container for up to 3 days.

"Peanut butter cups are some of my favorite candies, and they're right at home on top of these indulgent little cakes."—Paula

Strawberry Pound Cake

MAKES 1 (9-INCH) CAKE

Filled with juicy berries and topped with a layer of
crunchy sweetness, this potluck staple is a sight to behold.

¾ cup unsalted
   butter, softened
1¾ cups sugar, divided
 3 large eggs, room
   temperature
¾ teaspoon vanilla extract
2¼ cups all-purpose flour
1¾ teaspoons
   baking powder
½ teaspoon kosher salt
¾ cup sour cream, room
   temperature
 1 pound fresh
   strawberries, hulled

1 Preheat oven to 350°. Spray a 9-inch springform pan with baking spray with flour; line bottom of pan with parchment paper.

2 In the bowl of a stand mixer fitted with the paddle attachment, beat butter and 1½ cups sugar at medium speed until fluffy, 3 to 4 minutes, stopping to scrape sides of bowl. Add eggs, one at a time, beating well after each addition. Beat in vanilla.

3 In a medium bowl, whisk together flour, baking powder, and salt. With mixer on low speed, gradually add flour mixture to butter mixture alternately with sour cream, beginning and ending with flour mixture, beating just until combined after each addition.

4 Reserve 10 small strawberries. Chop remaining strawberries, and fold into batter. Spread batter in prepared pan.

5 Bake for 30 minutes. Carefully remove from oven. Cut reserved 10 strawberries in half, and arrange, cut side down, in top of batter. Sprinkle with remaining ¼ cup sugar. Bake until a wooden pick inserted in center comes out clean, about 1 hour more. Let cool completely in pan.

BAKING TIP

This recipe works in a springform pan only. It will not work in a regular
9-inch round cake pan. If you don't have a springform pan, the batter can
be divided and baked in 2 (9-inch) round cake pans or in a Bundt pan.

Chocolate Cherry Bundt Cake

This chocolate cola cake will be the cherry on top of your next cookout—I guarantee it.

Cake:

- 2 (15.25-ounce) boxes chocolate fudge cake mix
- 1½ cups cherry cola (not diet), room temperature
- 3 large eggs
- ½ cup vegetable oil
- ½ teaspoon almond extract
- ¾ cup chopped maraschino cherries, patted dry

Glaze:

- ½ cup cherry cola (not diet)
- ¼ cup unsalted butter
- ¼ teaspoon almond extract
- ½ cup bittersweet chocolate morsels
- 4 cups confectioners' sugar

1 Preheat oven to 350°. Spray a 15-cup Bundt pan with baking spray with flour.

2 **For cake:** In a large bowl, beat cake mixes, cola, eggs, oil, and extract with a mixer at medium speed until thick and smooth, about 2 minutes. Stir in cherries. Pour batter into prepared pan.

3 Bake until a wooden pick inserted near center comes out clean, about 50 minutes. Let cool in pan for 15 minutes. Remove from pan, and let cool completely on a wire rack.

4 **For glaze:** In a medium saucepan, bring cola, butter, and extract to a boil over medium-high heat, stirring until butter is melted. Remove from heat; stir in chocolate until melted.

5 Transfer chocolate mixture to a large bowl; with a mixer at medium speed, add confectioners' sugar, 1 cup at a time, beating until smooth. Drizzle onto cooled cake, and let stand until set, about 1 hour. Store in an airtight container for up to 3 days.

Glazed Clementine Cake

MAKES 1 (9-INCH) CAKE

Clementines have a sweet, thin skin, so you can
use the whole fruit in this cake for the best flavor.

Cake:
- 3 clementines
- 6 large eggs, room temperature
- 1 cup granulated sugar
- 1 teaspoon almond extract
- 2 cups blanched almond flour
- ½ cup plain yellow cornmeal
- 1½ teaspoons baking powder
- 1 teaspoon kosher salt

Glaze:
- 2 cups confectioners' sugar
- ¼ teaspoon clementine zest
- ¼ cup fresh clementine juice (about 2 clementines)

Garnish: clementine slices

1 Preheat oven to 350°. Spray a 9-inch round cake pan with baking spray with flour.

2 **For cake:** Place whole, unpeeled clementines in a medium microwave-safe bowl, and cover with plastic wrap. Microwave on high for 4 minutes. Carefully remove plastic wrap, and let cool for 10 minutes. Transfer clementines to the container of a blender; blend until smooth.

3 In a large bowl, beat eggs and granulated sugar with a mixer at high speed until mixture is pale yellow and almost doubled in volume, about 5 minutes. Whisk in clementine purée and extract. Stir in almond flour, cornmeal, baking powder, and salt. Spread batter into prepared pan.

4 Bake until a wooden pick inserted in center comes out clean, 30 to 35 minutes. Let cool in pan for 10 minutes. Remove from pan, and let cool completely on a wire rack.

5 **For glaze:** In a small bowl, whisk together all ingredients until smooth. Pour onto cooled cake. Garnish with clementine slices, if desired.

CHAPTER 5

Family Celebrations

Y'all know my family means the world to me, so I love any chance I get to celebrate them and the big moments in their lives. It just wouldn't be a birthday party, baby shower, or special Sunday supper without an impressive, festive dessert, and these recipes are some of my very best. Whether it's an occasion big or small, enjoy these delectable dishes that will be the stars of your family table.

Classic Angel Food Cake

This light and airy cake is the perfect blank canvas, and
my family likes to serve each slice with fresh seasonal fruit.

14 large egg whites,
   room temperature
 1 teaspoon cream of tartar
¼ teaspoon kosher salt
1¾ cups confectioners'
   sugar, divided
½ teaspoon lemon zest
½ teaspoon almond extract
½ teaspoon vanilla extract
1¼ cups cake flour
Sweetened whipped cream
   and fresh blackberries,
   to serve
Garnish: confectioners' sugar,
   lemon zest strips

1 Preheat oven to 350°.

2 In a large bowl, beat egg whites, cream of tartar, and salt with a mixer at high speed until foamy. Gradually add 1 cup confectioners' sugar, 1 tablespoon at a time, beating until stiff peaks form. Beat in zest and extracts.

3 In a medium bowl, sift together flour and remaining ¾ cup confectioners' sugar; gently fold into egg white mixture. Spoon batter into an ungreased 10-inch removable-bottom tube pan.

4 Bake until lightly browned, 30 to 35 minutes. Invert cake in pan onto the small end of a funnel or neck of a bottle, and let cool completely. Gently run a knife around edges of cake to release sides. Remove cake from pan. Serve with whipped cream and blackberries. Garnish with confectioners' sugar and zest, if desired.

Fresh Strawberry Layer Cake

MAKES 1 (9-INCH) CAKE

Sweet strawberries are such a glory, and their ruby-red color makes this dessert as pretty to look at as it is delicious to eat.

Cake:
2½ cups chopped fresh
    strawberries, divided
¾ cup unsalted
    butter, softened
1½ cups granulated sugar
1 teaspoon strawberry
    extract
½ teaspoon vanilla extract
3 large eggs, room
    temperature
¾ cup whole milk, room
    temperature
3 cups self-rising flour

Frosting:
1½ cups unsalted
    butter, softened
½ teaspoon strawberry
    extract
6¼ cups confectioners'
    sugar
⅛ teaspoon kosher salt

Garnish: fresh strawberries

1 Preheat oven to 350°. Spray 2 (9-inch) round tall-sided cake pans with baking spray with flour. Line pans with parchment paper.

2 **For cake:** In the container of a blender, process 1½ cups strawberries until smooth. Reserve ⅔ cup purée in a small bowl for frosting; reserve ⅓ cup purée for cake batter.

3 In a large bowl, beat butter, granulated sugar, and extracts with a mixer at medium speed until fluffy, 3 to 4 minutes, stopping to scrape sides of bowl. Add eggs, one at a time, beating well after each addition.

4 In a small bowl, stir together milk and reserved ⅓ cup strawberry purée. With mixer on low speed, gradually add flour to butter mixture alternately with milk mixture, beginning and ending with flour, beating just until combined after each addition. Fold in remaining 1 cup chopped strawberries. Divide batter between prepared pans. Gently tap pans on counter twice to release air bubbles.

5 Bake until a wooden pick inserted in center comes out clean, about 27 minutes. Let cool in pans for 10 minutes. Remove from pans, and let cool completely on wire racks.

6 **For frosting:** In a large bowl, beat butter and strawberry extract with a mixer at medium speed until creamy. Gradually add confectioners' sugar, ⅓ cup reserved strawberry purée, and salt, beating until smooth. Beat in remaining strawberry purée, 1 tablespoon at a time, to achieve a spreadable consistency, if needed.

7 Spread frosting between layers and on top and sides of cake; refrigerate for 30 minutes. Just before serving, garnish with strawberries, if desired.

Chocolate Raspberry Cake Roll

Watch the cake carefully so it doesn't overbake, and work quickly to roll it up while it's still hot. Those two things are key to help prevent cracking in your cake after it's filled and rerolled.

Cake:

- 4 large eggs, room temperature, separated
- ½ cup plus ⅓ cup granulated sugar, divided
- 1 teaspoon vanilla extract
- ½ cup all-purpose flour
- ⅓ cup unsweetened cocoa powder, plus more for sifting
- ½ teaspoon baking powder
- ¼ teaspoon baking soda
- ¼ teaspoon kosher salt
- ⅓ cup hot water
- 2 teaspoons instant coffee granules
- ¼ teaspoon cream of tartar

Filling:

- 1 (8-ounce) package cream cheese, softened
- ½ cup confectioners' sugar
- 1 teaspoon vanilla extract
- 1 (8-ounce) container frozen whipped topping, thawed
- ½ cup fresh raspberries
- ⅓ cup seedless raspberry preserves, room temperature

Prepared chocolate sauce, to serve
Garnish: fresh raspberries

1 Preheat oven to 350°. Spray a 15x10-inch rimmed baking sheet with baking spray with flour. Line pan with parchment paper.

2 For cake: In a large bowl, beat egg yolks, ⅓ cup granulated sugar, and vanilla with a mixer at medium speed until thick and pale, about 3 minutes. In a small bowl, whisk together flour, cocoa, baking powder, baking soda, and salt. In another small bowl, stir together ⅓ cup hot water and coffee granules until dissolved. Gradually add flour mixture to egg yolk mixture alternately with coffee mixture, beginning and ending with flour mixture, beating just until combined after each addition.

3 In another large bowl, using clean beaters, beat egg whites and cream of tartar with a mixer at medium speed until soft peaks form. Gradually add remaining ½ cup granulated sugar, beating at high speed until stiff peaks form. Gently fold egg white mixture into batter. Spread batter into prepared pan.

4 Bake until cake springs back when lightly touched in center, 10 to 12 minutes. (Do not overbake.)

5 Meanwhile, sift cocoa into a 15x10-inch rectangle on a clean dish towel. Immediately loosen cake from sides of pan, and turn out onto prepared towel. Gently peel off parchment paper. Sift cocoa onto cake. Starting at one short side, roll up cake and towel together, and place, seam side down, on a wire rack. Let cool completely.

6 For filling: In a large bowl, beat cream cheese, confectioners' sugar, and vanilla with a mixer at medium speed until smooth and creamy; stir in whipped topping until well combined. Gently fold in raspberries. Gently unroll cake, and spread with preserves. Spread cream cheese mixture onto preserves. Reroll cake without towel, and place, seam side down, on a serving platter. Refrigerate for 1 hour; trim edges with a serrated knife, if desired.

7 Just before serving, sift cocoa powder onto cake. Serve with chocolate sauce. Garnish with raspberries, if desired. Cover and refrigerate for up to 3 days.

Ice Cream Cone Cupcakes

— MAKES 18 —

What could be better than a cupcake in an ice cream cone? These are just plain ole fun, and my grandbabies love to help me make them.

Cupcakes:
18 ice cream cones
1 (9-ounce) box yellow cake mix
¼ cup chocolate instant pudding mix
¼ cup dark unsweetened cocoa powder
2 large eggs, room temperature
¾ cup whole milk
2 tablespoons unsalted butter, melted

Frosting:
1½ cups unsalted butter, softened
5 cups confectioners' sugar
1 tablespoon whole milk
1 teaspoon vanilla extract
¼ teaspoon kosher salt
Food coloring (optional)

Sprinkles
Maraschino cherries

1 Preheat oven to 350°.

2 **For cupcakes:** Place ice cream cones in 18 muffin cups. In a large bowl, whisk together cake mix, pudding mix, and cocoa. In a medium bowl, whisk together eggs, milk, and melted butter. Stir egg mixture into cake mix mixture until thick and smooth, about 2 minutes. Fill cones halfway to two-thirds full with batter.

3 Bake until a wooden pick inserted in center comes out clean, 20 to 25 minutes. Let cool completely.

4 **For frosting:** In a large bowl, beat butter with a mixer at medium speed until creamy. Reduce mixer speed to low. Gradually add confectioners' sugar, milk, vanilla, and salt, beating until well combined. Divide buttercream among small bowls, and tint with food coloring, if desired.

5 Spread or pipe frosting onto cupcakes, and top with sprinkles and cherries. Cover and refrigerate for up to 2 days.

Flourless Chocolate Raspberry Cake

MAKES 1 (8-INCH) CAKE

Tart-sweet raspberries are the perfect contrast to
this intensely rich and decadent brownie-like cake.

Cake:
- 2 (4-ounce) bars bittersweet chocolate, chopped
- 2 (4-ounce) bars semisweet chocolate, chopped
- 1½ cups unsalted butter, cubed
- 2⅔ cups granulated sugar
- 8 large eggs
- 2 teaspoons vanilla extract
- ¼ teaspoon kosher salt
- 1½ cups unsweetened cocoa powder, sifted

Filling:
- ½ cup unsalted butter, softened
- 1 cup confectioners' sugar
- 2 tablespoons seedless raspberry jam
- 1 tablespoon raspberry liqueur (optional)
- 2 cups fresh raspberries

Topping:
- ¾ cup cold heavy whipping cream
- 1 tablespoon confectioners' sugar

Garnish: fresh raspberries

1 Preheat oven to 350°. Spray 2 (8-inch) round cake pans with baking spray with flour. Line bottom of pans with parchment paper.

2 **For cake:** In the top of a double boiler, cook chocolates and butter over simmering water, stirring occasionally, until mixture is melted and smooth. Remove from heat.

3 In a large bowl, whisk together granulated sugar, eggs, vanilla, and salt until well combined. Slowly pour melted chocolate mixture into sugar mixture, whisking constantly until smooth. Stir in cocoa until combined. Divide batter between prepared pans.

4 Bake until a thin crust forms on top and center is set, about 25 minutes. Let cool in pans for 10 minutes. Remove from pans, and let cool completely on wire racks.

5 **For filling:** In a medium bowl, beat butter, confectioners' sugar, jam, and liqueur (if using) with a mixer at medium speed until smooth. Place one cake layer on a serving plate, and spread filling onto layer. Press raspberries into filling to form a solid layer, and top with remaining cake layer.

6 **For topping:** In a medium bowl, beat cream and confectioners' sugar with a mixer at high speed until stiff peaks form. Spread onto cake, and garnish with raspberries, if desired. Serve immediately, or cover and refrigerate for up to 2 days.

Strawberry Swirl Pound Cake

A fruity swirl and tangy glaze turn buttery pound cake into an elegant dessert.

1 cup unsalted
  butter, softened
1 (8-ounce) package
  cream cheese, softened
3 cups granulated sugar
4 large eggs, room
  temperature
1 teaspoon almond extract
½ teaspoon vanilla extract
4 cups all-purpose flour
1 tablespoon
  baking powder
½ cup plus 2 tablespoons
  whole buttermilk, divided
⅔ cup prepared strawberry
  glaze
2 cups confectioners' sugar
Garnish: fresh strawberries

—— BAKING TIP ——

You can find strawberry glaze
in the produce section of
grocery stores. It's similar in
consistency to lemon curd.

1 Preheat oven to 325°. Spray a 15-cup Bundt pan with baking spray with flour.

2 In the bowl of a stand mixer fitted with the paddle attachment, beat butter, cream cheese, and granulated sugar at medium speed until fluffy, 4 to 5 minutes, stopping to scrape sides of bowl. Add eggs, one at a time, beating just until combined after each addition. Beat in extracts.

3 In a large bowl, whisk together flour and baking powder. With mixer on low speed, gradually add flour mixture to butter mixture alternately with ½ cup buttermilk, beginning and ending with flour mixture, beating just until combined after each addition.

4 Pour one-third of batter into prepared pan. Dollop 8 rounded teaspoonfuls strawberry glaze onto batter, and swirl together with a wooden skewer. Repeat batter and glaze procedure once; top with remaining batter.

5 Bake until a wooden pick inserted near center comes out clean, about 70 minutes. Let cool in pan on a wire rack for 15 minutes. Remove from pan, and let cool completely on a wire rack.

6 In a small bowl, whisk together confectioners' sugar and remaining 2 tablespoons buttermilk until smooth; drizzle onto cooled cake. Garnish with strawberries, if desired. Cover and refrigerate for up to 3 days.

Sour Cream Cheesecake with Gingersnap Crust

I love the spiced cookie crust on this cheesecake.
It's a great contrast to the silky smooth filling.

2 cups crushed
  gingersnap cookies
¼ cup unsalted
  butter, melted
5 (8-ounce) packages
  cream cheese, softened
2⅓ cups sugar, divided
2 tablespoons
  all-purpose flour
2 teaspoons vanilla extract
4 large eggs, room
  temperature
⅓ cup heavy
  whipping cream
1½ cups sour cream
Prepared caramel sauce,
  to serve

1 Preheat oven to 350°. Spray a 9-inch springform pan with baking spray with flour. Wrap bottom and sides of pan in heavy-duty foil.

2 In a medium bowl, stir together crushed gingersnaps and melted butter. Press mixture into bottom of prepared pan.

3 Bake for 10 minutes. Let cool on a wire rack for 30 minutes. Reduce oven temperature to 325°.

4 In the bowl of a stand mixer fitted with the paddle attachment, beat cream cheese at medium speed until creamy, about 2 minutes, stopping to scrape sides of bowl. Gradually add 2 cups sugar, flour, and vanilla, beating until smooth. Add eggs, one at a time, beating just until combined after each addition. Beat in cream. Pour into prepared crust. Place cheesecake in a roasting pan. Pour enough hot water into roasting pan to reach about 1 inch up sides of springform pan. (Do not let water come above foil.)

5 Bake until center is just set when cheesecake is gently shaken, about 1 hour and 20 minutes. In a small bowl, stir together sour cream and remaining ⅓ cup sugar until sugar is dissolved; pour onto hot cheesecake, gently spreading to edges. Turn oven off, and leave cheesecake in oven with door closed for 2 hours.

6 Remove cheesecake from oven and water bath. Remove foil from bottom and sides of pan, and let cheesecake cool completely on a wire rack. Run a knife around sides of pan. Loosely cover, and refrigerate until cold before serving, at least 4 hours or up to 3 days. Serve with caramel sauce.

Yellow Birthday Cake

Birthdays are a big deal in my family. This delicious cake is worthy of a special celebration.

Cake:
- 1⅓ cups unsalted butter, softened
- 2¾ cups granulated sugar
- 1 tablespoon vanilla extract
- 6 large eggs, room temperature
- 4 cups all-purpose flour
- 1 tablespoon baking powder
- ½ teaspoon baking soda
- 1½ cups whole buttermilk, room temperature
- ½ cup sour cream

Frosting:
- 3 (4-ounce) bars semisweet chocolate, chopped
- ¾ cup unsalted butter
- 1 cup sour cream
- 6 cups confectioners' sugar
- ¼ cup whole milk

Garnish: sprinkles

1 Preheat oven to 350°. Spray 2 (9-inch) round cake pans with baking spray with flour.

2 **For cake:** In a large bowl, beat butter, granulated sugar, and vanilla with a mixer at medium speed until fluffy, 3 to 4 minutes, stopping to scrape sides of bowl. Add eggs, one at a time, beating well after each addition.

3 In another large bowl, whisk together flour, baking powder, and baking soda. With mixer on low speed, gradually add flour mixture to butter mixture alternately with buttermilk, beginning and ending with flour mixture, beating just until combined after each addition. Stir in sour cream. Divide batter between prepared pans.

4 Bake until a wooden pick inserted in center comes out clean, about 45 minutes. Let cool in pans for 10 minutes. Remove from pans, and let cool completely on wire racks.

5 **For frosting:** In a small saucepan, cook chocolate and butter over medium-low heat, stirring frequently, until mixture is melted and smooth. Remove from heat; let cool for 45 minutes.

6 In a large bowl, beat chocolate mixture and sour cream with a mixer at low speed until combined. Gradually add confectioners' sugar, beating until smooth. Add milk, beating until combined. Spread frosting between layers and on top and sides of cake. Garnish with sprinkles, if desired. Cover and refrigerate for up to 3 days.

"Use this frosting as soon as you make it because it firms up as it stands." —Paula

Orange Ginger Carrot Cake

MAKES 1 (9-INCH) CAKE

This favorite Southern cake graces my family table year-round, and it tastes even better the day after it's made.

Cake:

1¼ cups granulated sugar
1 cup vegetable oil
4 large eggs, room temperature
1 tablespoon orange zest
2 cups all-purpose flour
2 teaspoons baking powder
2 teaspoons ground ginger
1 teaspoon baking soda
1 teaspoon kosher salt
1 teaspoon ground cinnamon
¼ teaspoon ground nutmeg
3 cups finely shredded carrot

Frosting:

1 cup unsalted butter, softened
1 (8-ounce) package cream cheese, softened
6 cups confectioners' sugar
1½ teaspoons orange zest
2 teaspoons fresh orange juice

Garnish: chopped toasted pecans

1 Preheat oven to 350°. Spray 2 (9-inch) round cake pans with baking spray with flour.

2 For cake: In a large bowl, beat granulated sugar, oil, and eggs with a mixer at medium-high speed until combined, 3 to 4 minutes, stopping to scrape sides of bowl. Add zest, beating until combined.

3 In a medium bowl, whisk together flour, baking powder, ginger, baking soda, salt, cinnamon, and nutmeg. With mixer on low speed, gradually add flour mixture to sugar mixture, beating until combined. Beat in carrot. Divide batter between prepared pans.

4 Bake until a wooden pick inserted in center comes out clean, about 23 minutes. Let cool in pans for 10 minutes. Remove from pans, and let cool completely on wire racks.

5 For frosting: In a large bowl, beat butter and cream cheese with a mixer at medium speed until creamy. Gradually add confectioners' sugar, beating until smooth. Beat in orange zest and juice. Spread frosting between layers and on top and sides of cake. Press pecans onto sides of cake, if desired. Cover and refrigerate for at least 3 hours before serving or up to 2 days.

Lemon Coconut Cake

This gorgeous cake is an ideal centerpiece for any Southern dessert buffet.

Cake:
- 1 cup unsalted butter, softened
- 2 cups granulated sugar
- 4 large eggs, room temperature
- 3½ cups cake flour
- 1 tablespoon baking powder
- 1 (8.5-ounce) can cream of coconut
- ½ cup whole buttermilk
- 2 teaspoons vanilla extract

Frosting:
- 1 cup unsalted butter, softened
- 1 (2-pound) bag confectioners' sugar
- 8 to 9 tablespoons whole milk
- 2 teaspoons vanilla extract

Filling:
- 1 cup granulated sugar
- ¼ cup cornstarch
- 1 cup fresh lemon juice
- 4 large egg yolks
- ½ cup unsalted butter, cubed and softened

Garnish: sweetened flaked coconut, fresh lemon wedges

1 Preheat oven to 350°. Spray 2 (9-inch) round cake pans with baking spray with flour.

2 **For cake:** In a large bowl, beat butter and granulated sugar with a mixer at medium speed until fluffy, 4 to 5 minutes, stopping to scrape sides of bowl. Add eggs, one at a time, beating well after each addition.

3 In another large bowl, whisk together flour and baking powder. In a small bowl, whisk together cream of coconut, buttermilk, and vanilla. With mixer on low speed, gradually add flour mixture to butter mixture alternately with cream of coconut mixture, beginning and ending with flour mixture, beating just until combined after each addition. Spread batter into prepared pans.

4 Bake until a wooden pick inserted in center comes out clean, 25 to 30 minutes. Let cool in pans for 10 minutes. Remove from pans, and let cool completely on wire racks.

5 **For frosting:** In a large bowl, beat butter and confectioners' sugar with a mixer at medium speed until smooth and creamy, stopping to scrape sides of bowl. Add milk, 1 tablespoon at a time, beating until a spreadable consistency is reached. Beat in vanilla.

6 **For filling:** In a 3-quart saucepan, whisk together granulated sugar and cornstarch. Whisk in lemon juice until cornstarch is dissolved and mixture is smooth. Cook over medium heat, whisking constantly, until mixture is hot.

7 In a medium bowl, whisk egg yolks. Whisking constantly, slowly add one-fourth of hot lemon mixture to yolks. Whisk egg mixture into lemon mixture, and cook, whisking constantly, until thickened, 10 to 12 minutes. Remove from heat, and whisk in butter, a few pieces at a time, until melted and smooth. Pour mixture into a large bowl, and cover with a piece of plastic wrap, pressing wrap directly onto surface to prevent a skin from forming. Refrigerate until thickened and cold, about 4 hours or up to 3 days.

8 Place one cake layer on a serving platter, and pipe a thin layer of frosting around edge of cake. Spread 1 cup filling onto cake layer inside frosting border. Top with remaining cake layer. Spread remaining frosting on top and sides of cake. Spread remaining filling on top of cake. Press coconut onto sides of cake, and garnish with lemon wedges, if desired. Cover and refrigerate for up to 3 days.

CHAPTER 6

Harvest Favorites

When fall is just around the corner, I get excited to bake with the cozy flavors of the season. Pumpkin, apple, sweet potato, cranberry, and more fill my favorite recipes and remind me of baking with my boys for family holidays. In this chapter, you'll find pies filled with all kinds of fruits and spices, decadent cakes with crunchy toppings and creamy frostings, and comforting breads and bars that will satisfy every autumn craving.

Pumpkin Pie

A sweet and simple homemade pumpkin
pie is a must-have recipe all autumn long.

Crust:
1¼ cups all-purpose flour
 1 teaspoon kosher salt
 1 teaspoon granulated sugar
 ½ cup cold unsalted butter,
   cubed
3 to 4 tablespoons cold
   whole buttermilk

Filling:
 1 (15-ounce) can pumpkin
 3 large eggs
 1 cup half-and-half
 ¾ cup firmly packed
   light brown sugar
 2 tablespoons
   all-purpose flour
1½ teaspoons ground
   cinnamon
 1 teaspoon ground ginger
 ½ teaspoon kosher salt
 ¼ teaspoon ground allspice
 ¼ teaspoon ground nutmeg

Sweetened whipped cream,
   to serve

1 Preheat oven to 350°.

2 **For crust:** In a medium bowl, whisk together flour, salt, and granulated sugar. Using a pastry blender, cut in cold butter until mixture is crumbly. Add cold buttermilk, 1 tablespoon at a time, stirring until a dough forms. Turn out dough, and shape into a disk. Wrap tightly in plastic wrap, and refrigerate for 30 minutes.

3 On a lightly floured surface, roll dough into a 12-inch circle. Transfer to a 9-inch pie plate, pressing into bottom and up sides. Trim excess dough. Fold edges under, and crimp as desired. Freeze for 10 minutes.

4 **For filling:** In a large bowl, whisk together all ingredients until smooth. Pour into prepared crust. Place pie on a baking sheet.

5 Bake until center is set, about 1 hour, covering with foil after 30 minutes to prevent excess browning, if necessary. Let cool completely on a wire rack. Serve with whipped cream. Cover and refrigerate for up to 3 days.

"It's always a toss-up for me between pumpkin pie and sweet potato pie— I say have both!"—Paula

Spiced Cranberry Pecan Bars

I love this vibrant cranberry filling, and the crumbly topping on these bars adds the perfect buttery touch.

Crust:
- 2½ cups all-purpose flour
- ½ cup sugar
- 1½ teaspoons apple pie spice
- ¾ teaspoon baking powder
- ½ teaspoon ground ginger
- ½ teaspoon kosher salt
- 1 cup cold unsalted butter, cubed
- 1 large egg

Filling:
- 5 cups fresh cranberries, divided
- ¾ cup sugar
- ½ cup applesauce
- ½ cup maple syrup
- 2 tablespoons orange zest
- 2 tablespoons fresh orange juice
- ¼ teaspoon kosher salt
- 1½ tablespoons cornstarch
- 1½ tablespoons water

Topping:
- ½ cup chopped pecans
- ½ cup old-fashioned oats

1 Preheat oven to 350°. Line a 13x9-inch baking dish with parchment paper, letting excess extend over sides of pan.

2 **For crust:** In a large bowl, whisk together flour, sugar, pie spice, baking powder, ginger, and salt. Add cold butter, and beat with a mixer at medium speed until crumbly. Add egg, beating until combined. Reserve 1 cup mixture for topping; press remaining mixture into bottom of prepared pan.

3 Bake until lightly golden, about 18 minutes.

4 **For filling:** In a large saucepan, bring 3 cups cranberries, sugar, applesauce, maple syrup, orange zest and juice, and salt to a boil over medium-high heat. Cook, stirring constantly, until cranberries begin to burst. Reduce heat to low, and simmer, stirring occasionally, for 10 minutes.

5 In a small bowl, whisk together cornstarch and 1½ tablespoons water; stir into cranberry mixture, and cook until thickened, about 2 minutes. Remove from heat; fold in remaining 2 cups cranberries. Spread mixture in an even layer onto prepared crust.

6 **For topping:** In a small bowl, combine pecans, oats, and reserved 1 cup crust mixture. Sprinkle onto filling.

7 Bake until topping is golden and filling is bubbly, about 30 minutes. Let cool completely on a wire rack. Using excess parchment as handles, remove from pan, and cut into bars. Store in an airtight container for up to 3 days.

Caramel Apple Crisp Bars

These bars combine the best of buttery apple pie,
juicy apple cobbler, and gooey caramel apples.

3 large Granny Smith apples, peeled, halved, and sliced ¼ inch thick

3 large Honeycrisp apples, peeled, halved, and sliced ¼ inch thick

1 cup granulated sugar, divided

3⅔ cups all-purpose flour, divided

3 cups old-fashioned oats

1¾ cups unsalted butter, softened

1½ cups plus ⅔ cup firmly packed light brown sugar, divided

2½ teaspoons kosher salt, divided

1¼ teaspoons baking soda

1 cup chopped pecans

2 tablespoons cornstarch

1 tablespoon ground cinnamon

2 teaspoons vanilla extract

½ teaspoon ground nutmeg

1 (11-ounce) bag individually wrapped caramel candies, unwrapped

2 tablespoons heavy whipping cream

1 In a large bowl, stir together apples and ½ cup granulated sugar. Let stand for 30 minutes.

2 Preheat oven to 350°. Line a 13x9-inch baking pan with heavy-duty foil, letting excess extend over sides of pan. Spray foil with cooking spray.

3 In a large bowl, beat 3 cups flour, oats, butter, 1½ cups brown sugar, 1½ teaspoons salt, and baking soda with a mixer at medium speed until well combined and crumbly. Press 4 cups oat mixture into bottom of prepared pan; stir pecans into remaining oat mixture, and reserve.

4 Drain apples, discarding liquid. Add cornstarch, cinnamon, vanilla, nutmeg, remaining ⅔ cup flour, remaining ⅔ cup brown sugar, remaining 1 teaspoon salt, and remaining ½ cup granulated sugar to apples, stirring until well combined.

5 Bake crust for 20 minutes. Let cool for 5 minutes. Leave oven on.

6 Spread apple mixture onto hot crust, and sprinkle with reserved oat mixture. Bake 40 minutes more. Let cool completely in pan on a wire rack. Refrigerate until firm, 2 to 3 hours.

7 Using excess foil as handles, remove from pan, and cut into bars. In a medium microwave-safe bowl, heat caramels and cream on high in 15-second intervals, stirring between each, until melted and smooth (about 1 minute total). Drizzle caramel onto bars, and let stand until set, about 5 minutes. Cover and refrigerate for up to 3 days.

Pumpkin Whoopie Pies

Pumpkin and plenty of warm spices give
these classic snack cakes a hint of fall flair.

Cookies:
- 1 cup unsalted
  butter, softened
- 2 cups firmly packed
  light brown sugar
- 1 (15-ounce) can pumpkin
- 1 teaspoon vanilla extract
- 2 large eggs, room
  temperature
- 3 cups all-purpose flour
- 1 teaspoon baking soda
- 1 teaspoon ground cinnamon
- ½ teaspoon baking powder
- ½ teaspoon kosher salt
- ¼ teaspoon ground ginger
- ¼ teaspoon ground nutmeg
- ⅛ teaspoon ground allspice
- ⅛ teaspoon ground cloves

Filling:
- 1 cup unsalted
  butter, softened
- 2 cups confectioners' sugar
- ⅔ cup maple syrup
- ½ teaspoon vanilla extract
- ½ teaspoon kosher salt
- ½ teaspoon ground
  cinnamon

1 Preheat oven to 350°. Line baking sheets with parchment paper.

2 **For cookies:** In a large bowl, beat butter and brown sugar with a mixer at medium speed until fluffy, 3 to 4 minutes, stopping to scrape sides of bowl. Beat in pumpkin and vanilla. Add eggs, one at a time, beating well after each addition.

3 In another large bowl, whisk together flour, baking soda, cinnamon, baking powder, salt, ginger, nutmeg, allspice, and cloves. With mixer on low speed, gradually add flour mixture to butter mixture, beating until combined. Using a 1½-tablespoon spring-loaded scoop, drop batter 2 inches apart onto prepared pans.

4 Bake until a wooden pick inserted in center comes out clean, 10 to 12 minutes. Let cool on pans for 5 minutes. Remove from pans, and let cool completely on wire racks.

5 **For filling:** In a medium bowl, beat butter and confectioners' sugar with a mixer at medium speed until fluffy, about 2 minutes, stopping to scrape sides of bowl. With mixer on low speed, add maple syrup and vanilla, beating until combined. Add salt and cinnamon, beating until light and fluffy, 5 to 6 minutes.

6 Spread or pipe filling onto flat side of half of cookies. Place remaining cookies, flat side down, onto filling, pressing gently. Store in an airtight container for up to 3 days.

Streusel-Topped Pumpkin Swirl Cheesecake

—— MAKES 1 (9-INCH) CAKE ——

A pecan and brown sugar streusel tops my favorite autumnal cheesecake.
A drizzle of rich butterscotch sauce makes it irresistible.

Crust:
- 1½ cups graham cracker crumbs
- ⅓ cup unsalted butter, melted
- ¼ cup granulated sugar
- ⅛ teaspoon kosher salt

Filling:
- 5 (8-ounce) packages cream cheese, softened and divided
- ¾ cup granulated sugar, divided
- ½ cup firmly packed light brown sugar
- 1 (15-ounce) can pumpkin
- 2 tablespoons all-purpose flour
- 1 tablespoon pumpkin pie spice
- 2 teaspoons vanilla extract
- 5 large eggs, room temperature, divided

Topping:
- ½ cup chopped toasted pecans
- ⅓ cup all-purpose flour
- ¼ cup granulated sugar
- ¼ cup firmly packed light brown sugar
- 3 tablespoons unsalted butter, melted
- ⅛ teaspoon kosher salt

Prepared butterscotch sauce, to serve

1 Preheat oven to 325°. Spray a 9-inch springform pan with baking spray with flour.

2 For crust: In a medium bowl, stir together all ingredients. Press mixture into bottom of prepared pan. Place pan on a rimmed baking sheet.

3 Bake for 7 minutes. Let cool on a wire rack. Leave oven on.

4 For filling: In a large bowl, beat 4 packages cream cheese with a mixer at medium speed until creamy. Add ½ cup granulated sugar and brown sugar, beating until smooth. Reduce mixer speed to low, and add pumpkin, flour, pie spice, and vanilla, beating until well combined. Add 4 eggs, one at a time, beating just until combined after each addition. Pour half of pumpkin mixture into prepared crust.

5 In a medium bowl, beat remaining package cream cheese with a mixer at medium speed until creamy. Add remaining ¼ cup granulated sugar, beating until combined. Beat in remaining egg until smooth. Gently spread cream cheese mixture onto pumpkin filling in pan, leaving a 1-inch border around sides of pan. Gently pour remaining pumpkin mixture onto cream cheese mixture. Return pan to baking sheet.

6 Bake for 1 hour.

7 For topping: In a medium bowl, stir together all ingredients until large pieces form; sprinkle onto cheesecake. Bake 15 minutes more. Let cool in pan on a wire rack for 2 hours. Loosely cover, and refrigerate for at least 8 hours before serving or for up to 3 days. Serve with butterscotch sauce.

Bourbon Pecan Pie

Calling all pecan pie fans—this version has all the crunchy nuts and gooey filling you crave, along with a healthy splash of the South's favorite spirit.

½ (14.1-ounce) package refrigerated piecrusts
2 cups pecan halves and pieces
⅔ cup firmly packed light brown sugar
⅔ cup dark corn syrup
6 tablespoons unsalted butter, melted
3 large eggs, lightly beaten
3 tablespoons bourbon
½ teaspoon kosher salt

1 Preheat oven to 350°.

2 On a lightly floured surface, unroll one piecrust. Transfer to a 9-inch pie plate, pressing into bottom and up sides. Fold edges under, and crimp as desired. Refrigerate for 10 minutes.

3 Sprinkle pecans into prepared crust. In a large bowl, whisk together brown sugar, corn syrup, melted butter, eggs, bourbon, and salt until almost foamy. Pour filling onto pecans.

4 Bake until top is almost set, 45 to 50 minutes, covering with foil to prevent excess browning. Let cool completely on a wire rack.

Apple Cranberry Cobbler

MAKES 6 TO 8 SERVINGS

Pop this cobbler in the oven about an hour before you sit down to supper; it'll bake and cool to perfection while you eat.

5 cups thinly sliced peeled
  Granny Smith apples
  (about 5 medium apples)
3 cups thinly sliced peeled Gala
  apples (about 3 medium apples)
2 cups fresh or thawed frozen
  cranberries
2 cups plus 2 tablespoons
  all-purpose flour, divided
2 tablespoons firmly packed
  dark brown sugar
1 tablespoon fresh orange juice
1 teaspoon apple pie spice
2 cups granulated sugar
1 teaspoon kosher salt
2 large eggs
¾ cup cold unsalted butter, cubed

1 Preheat oven to 375°. Spray a 13x9-inch baking dish with baking spray with flour.

2 In a large bowl, stir together apples, cranberries, 2 tablespoons flour, brown sugar, orange juice, and pie spice until well combined. Spread into prepared pan.

3 In a medium bowl, whisk together granulated sugar, salt, and remaining 2 cups flour. Whisk in eggs. Using a pastry blender, cut in cold butter until mixture is crumbly. Sprinkle onto fruit mixture.

4 Bake until golden brown and bubbly, 45 to 55 minutes, loosely covering with foil to prevent excess browning, if necessary. Let cool for 30 minutes; serve warm.

Glazed Maple Pecan Coffee Cake

MAKES 1 (10-INCH) CAKE

Skip making endless batches of pancakes for weekend breakfasts, and bake this cake instead. It tastes just like a tall stack of flapjacks.

Topping:
- 1 cup all-purpose flour
- ½ cup firmly packed light brown sugar
- ¼ teaspoon kosher salt
- 6 tablespoons unsalted butter, melted
- ½ cup chopped pecans

Cake:
- 1 (15.25-ounce) box butter pecan cake mix
- 3 large eggs
- 1 cup apple juice
- ½ cup vegetable oil
- ¼ cup all-purpose flour
- ½ teaspoon maple extract

Glaze:
- 2 ounces cream cheese, softened
- 1 tablespoon unsalted butter, softened
- ⅓ cup confectioners' sugar
- ¼ cup whole buttermilk

1 Preheat oven to 350°. Spray a 10-inch springform pan with baking spray with flour.

2 **For topping:** In a medium bowl, whisk together flour, brown sugar, and salt. Stir in butter until large crumbs form; stir in pecans. Refrigerate until ready to use.

3 **For cake:** In a large bowl, beat all ingredients with a mixer until thick and smooth, about 3 minutes, stopping to scrape sides of bowl. Spread batter into prepared pan. Sprinkle topping in large crumbs onto batter.

4 Bake for 40 minutes. Loosely cover with foil, and bake until a wooden pick inserted in center comes out clean, 10 to 15 minutes more. Let cool in pan on a wire rack for 20 minutes. Remove sides of springform pan, and let cake cool slightly.

5 **For glaze:** In a small bowl, beat cream cheese and butter with a mixer on medium speed until smooth. Beat in confectioners' sugar until combined. Gradually beat in buttermilk until smooth. Drizzle onto warm cake; serve warm.

"This rich glaze is so good, you'll want to eat it by the spoonful!"—Paula

Fried Apple Hand Pies

I adore hand pies. I've made them just about every way, but these are my absolute favorite.

Dough:

2½ cups all-purpose flour
2 teaspoons kosher salt
2 teaspoons granulated sugar
1 cup cold unsalted butter, cubed
1 tablespoon apple cider vinegar
4 to 6 tablespoons ice water

Filling:

3 cups chopped peeled Granny Smith apples (about 3 large)
⅔ cup firmly packed light brown sugar
2 tablespoons unsalted butter
2 teaspoons ground cinnamon
1 teaspoon fresh lemon juice
1 tablespoon apple cider or apple juice
2 teaspoons cornstarch

Canola oil, for frying
Confectioners' sugar, for sifting

1 **For dough:** In the work bowl of a food processor, place flour, salt, and granulated sugar; pulse until combined. Add cold butter, and pulse until mixture is crumbly. Gradually add vinegar and ice water, 1 tablespoon at a time, pulsing just until a dough forms. Turn out dough onto a lightly floured surface, and divide in half. Shape each half into a disk, and wrap in plastic wrap. Refrigerate until firm, 30 to 45 minutes.

2 **For filling:** In a large skillet, cook apples, brown sugar, butter, cinnamon, and lemon juice over medium-high heat, stirring occasionally, until apples are tender, 6 to 8 minutes. In a small bowl, whisk together apple cider or juice and cornstarch until smooth; stir into apple mixture. Cook until slightly thickened, about 1 minute. Let cool completely.

3 In a large Dutch oven, pour oil to a depth of 3 inches, and heat over medium heat until a deep-fry thermometer registers 350°.

4 On a lightly floured surface, roll each dough disk to ⅛-inch thickness. Using an inverted cereal bowl, cut 5½-inch circles from dough, gently rerolling scraps to use all dough. Spoon 2 heaping tablespoonfuls apple mixture into center of each dough circle. Brush edges of dough with water. Fold dough over apples, and press edges with a fork to seal. Freeze pies until cold, about 5 minutes.

5 Fry pies, two at a time, turning occasionally, until golden brown, about 5 minutes. Let drain on paper towels. Sift with confectioners' sugar before serving.

Sweet Potato Pie with Meringue Topping

I adore sweet potato pie, and the mile-high meringue takes it over the top.

Crust:

1½ (7-ounce) packages amaretti cookies, crushed
⅓ cup unsalted butter, melted
⅛ teaspoon kosher salt

Filling:

4 large eggs
1 cup sugar
1 teaspoon pumpkin pie spice
1 teaspoon vanilla extract
¾ teaspoon kosher salt
2 cups mashed cooked sweet potato (about 2 large sweet potatoes)

Topping:

1 cup sugar
¼ cup water
2 tablespoons light corn syrup
3 egg whites, room temperature
⅛ teaspoon kosher salt
⅛ teaspoon cream of tartar

1 Preheat oven to 375°.

2 **For crust:** In a medium bowl, whisk together all ingredients. Using the bottom of a measuring cup, press mixture into bottom and up sides of a 9-inch pie plate.

3 Bake for 10 minutes. Let cool on a wire rack. Reduce oven temperature to 350°.

4 **For filling:** In a large bowl, whisk together eggs, sugar, pie spice, vanilla, and salt until smooth; whisk in sweet potato until well combined. Spread filling into prepared crust. Cover edges of crust with foil.

5 Bake until an instant-read thermometer inserted in center registers 200°, 45 to 55 minutes. Let cool completely on a wire rack.

6 **For topping:** In a large heavy-bottomed saucepan, stir together sugar, ¼ cup water, and corn syrup just until moistened. Cook over medium-high heat, without stirring, until mixture registers 240° on a candy thermometer, about 16 minutes. Remove from heat; let cool just until mixture stops boiling.

7 Meanwhile, in a large bowl, beat egg whites, salt, and cream of tartar with a mixer at medium speed until soft peaks form. Increase mixer speed to high, and gradually add hot sugar syrup in a slow, steady stream. Beat until mixture is thick, white, and glossy, 4 to 6 minutes. Spread meringue onto pie, sealing edges. Using a handheld kitchen torch, carefully brown meringue. Serve immediately.

Pecan Pie Cake

MAKES 1 (9-INCH) CAKE

My family enjoys slice after slice of this ooey-gooey cake.

Cake:
- 1½ cups unsalted butter, softened
- 2 cups granulated sugar
- 6 large eggs, room temperature, separated
- 3¼ cups all-purpose flour
- 1 teaspoon baking soda
- 1 teaspoon kosher salt
- 1 cup sour cream
- 3 tablespoons whole milk
- 1 teaspoon vanilla extract

Filling:
- 1½ cups chopped pecans
- 1 cup granulated sugar
- ⅔ cup light corn syrup
- ⅓ cup unsalted butter
- 2 large eggs, beaten
- ¼ teaspoon kosher salt
- 1 teaspoon vanilla extract

Frosting:
- 1 cup firmly packed dark brown sugar
- ⅓ cup water
- ½ teaspoon kosher salt
- 1 cup unsalted butter, softened and divided
- 1 (8-ounce) package cream cheese, softened
- 1 (2-pound) bag confectioners' sugar
- 1 to 3 tablespoons whole milk

Garnish: prepared caramel sauce, pecan halves

1 Preheat oven to 350°. Spray 3 (9-inch) round cake pans with baking spray with flour. Line bottom of pans with parchment paper.

2 For cake: In a large bowl, beat butter and granulated sugar with a mixer at medium speed until fluffy, 3 to 4 minutes, stopping to scrape sides of bowl. Add egg yolks, one at a time, beating well after each addition.

3 In a medium bowl, whisk together flour, baking soda, and salt. In a small bowl, stir together sour cream, milk, and vanilla. With mixer on low speed, gradually add flour mixture to butter mixture alternately with sour cream mixture, beginning and ending with flour mixture, beating just until combined after each addition.

4 In another large bowl, using clean beaters, beat egg whites with a mixer at high speed until stiff peaks form. Stir one-third of egg whites into batter; gently fold in remaining egg whites. Divide batter among prepared pans.

5 Bake until a wooden pick inserted in center comes out clean, about 20 minutes. Let cool in pans for 10 minutes. Remove from pans, and let cool completely on wire racks.

6 For filling: In a medium saucepan, stir together pecans, granulated sugar, corn syrup, butter, eggs, and salt until well combined; bring to a boil over medium-high heat. Reduce heat, and simmer, stirring constantly, until thickened, 6 to 8 minutes. Remove from heat; stir in vanilla. Let cool completely.

7 For frosting: In a small saucepan, bring brown sugar, ⅓ cup water, and salt to a boil over medium-high heat, stirring constantly, until sugar is dissolved. Remove from heat; stir in ½ cup butter. Let cool completely.

8 In a large bowl, beat cooled sugar mixture, cream cheese, and remaining ½ cup butter with a mixer at medium speed until creamy. Reduce mixer speed to low. Gradually add confectioners' sugar, beating until smooth. If frosting is too thick to spread, add milk, 1 tablespoon at a time, beating until a spreadable consistency is reached.

9 Spread filling between cake layers. Spread filling on top and sides of cake. Garnish with caramel and pecans, if desired. Cover and refrigerate for up to 3 days.

Rustic Apple Tart

Apples are a fall staple in my kitchen, and this
tart makes the most of their subtly sweet flavor.

1 (14.1-ounce) package
refrigerated piecrusts
2 pounds Golden Delicious
apples, peeled, cored,
and thinly sliced (about
6 medium apples)
2 tablespoons plus
2 teaspoons sugar, divided
1 teaspoon apple pie spice
¾ teaspoon cornstarch
1 large egg
1 tablespoon water

BAKING TIP

Apple varieties well suited for
baking include Braeburn, Gala,
Golden Delicious, Granny Smith,
Honeycrisp, Pink Lady, and Rome.

1 Preheat oven to 400°.

2 On a lightly floured surface, unroll one piecrust. Place remaining crust on top, pressing to seal layers; roll into a 14-inch circle. Transfer to a 10-inch removable-bottom fluted tart pan, pressing into bottom and sides; let excess crust extend over sides of pan.

3 Place apple slices onto crust, fanning out decoratively. In a small bowl, whisk together 2 tablespoons sugar, pie spice, and cornstarch; sprinkle onto apples. Fold excess dough over apples, and pleat edges.

4 In a small bowl, whisk together egg and 1 tablespoon water; brush onto dough, and sprinkle with remaining 2 teaspoons sugar. Place tart pan on a baking sheet.

5 Bake for 30 minutes. Cover with foil, and bake until crust is golden brown and apples are tender, 10 to 15 minutes more. Let cool in pan on a wire rack for 10 minutes. Remove from pan, and let cool completely on wire rack.

Deep-Dish Apple Pear Pie

This pie is filled to the brim with juicy apples and pears.

2½ pounds Anjou pears, peeled, cored, and sliced ¼ inch thick (about 5 medium pears)

1½ pounds Granny Smith apples, peeled, cored, and sliced ¼ inch thick (about 5 medium apples)

1 pound Gala apples, peeled, cored, and sliced ¼ inch thick (about 3 medium apples)

⅔ cup granulated sugar

⅓ cup firmly packed light brown sugar

2 lemons, juiced

1 (14.1-ounce) package refrigerated piecrusts

5 tablespoons all-purpose flour

1½ teaspoons ground cinnamon

4 tablespoons unsalted butter, cubed and divided

1 In a large bowl, stir together pears, apples, sugars, and lemon juice. Let stand for 30 minutes.

2 Preheat oven to 350°.

3 On a lightly floured surface, roll 1 piecrust into an 11-inch circle. Transfer to a 9-inch deep-dish pie plate, pressing into bottom and up sides.

4 Drain fruit mixture well, discarding liquid. In a small bowl, whisk together flour and cinnamon. Stir flour mixture into fruit mixture until well combined. Spread half of fruit mixture into prepared crust. Dot 2 tablespoons butter onto fruit mixture. Repeat with remaining fruit mixture and remaining 2 tablespoons butter.

5 On a lightly floured surface, roll remaining piecrust into an 11-inch circle. Using a small leaf-shaped cutter, cut 3 leaves from center of crust. (Reserve leaves.) Lightly brush water onto edges of bottom crust, and gently place cutout crust over fruit. Fold edges under, and crimp as desired. Lightly brush one side of leaves with water, and place on top crust opposite cuts in crust. Cover edges of crust with foil.

6 Bake on lowest oven rack until crust is golden brown and filling is bubbly, about 1 hour. Let cool on a wire rack for at least 1 hour before serving. Store in an airtight container for up to 3 days.

Spiced Banana Bread Crisp

MAKES 6 TO 8 SERVINGS

This quick crisp might use convenience products, but that doesn't mean it skimps on flavor. After just one bite, you'll be reaching for another scoop.

1 (15.25-ounce) box
  spice cake mix
1 cup whole milk
½ cup butterscotch morsels
½ cup unsalted butter, melted
6 medium bananas, sliced
1¼ cups firmly packed dark
  brown sugar, divided
½ cup warm water
1 teaspoon ground cinnamon
1 cup old-fashioned oats
½ cup self-rising flour
½ cup chopped pecans
½ cup unsalted butter, softened
Vanilla ice cream, to serve
Garnish: sliced bananas,
  chopped pecans

1 Preheat oven to 375°. Spray a 13x9-inch baking dish with baking spray with flour.

2 In a large bowl, stir together cake mix, milk, butterscotch morsels, and melted butter until well combined. Spread into prepared pan. Layer with banana slices.

3 In a small bowl, whisk together ½ cup brown sugar, ½ cup warm water, and cinnamon until well combined. Slowly pour onto bananas.

4 In a medium bowl, stir together oats, flour, pecans, softened butter, and remaining ¾ cup brown sugar until well combined and crumbly. Sprinkle onto bananas.

5 Bake until golden brown and bubbly, 40 to 45 minutes. Let cool for 20 to 30 minutes; serve with ice cream, and garnish with bananas and pecans, if desired.

Cranberry and Rosemary Biscuits

MAKES 8

These sweet and savory biscuits are crispy on the outside and tender within.
They'll be a great addition to your family Thanksgiving feast.

3 cups all-purpose flour

3 tablespoons sugar

1½ tablespoons baking powder

1 tablespoon chopped
  fresh rosemary

1½ teaspoons kosher salt

1½ teaspoons ground
  black pepper

¾ teaspoon baking soda

⅔ cup cold unsalted butter,
  cubed

1¼ cups fresh cranberries

1 cup shredded Gruyère cheese

1½ cups plus 2 tablespoons cold
  whole buttermilk, divided

Garnish: flaked sea salt

1 Preheat oven to 350°. Line a baking sheet with parchment paper. In a large bowl, stir together flour, sugar, baking powder, rosemary, salt, pepper, and baking soda. Using a pastry blender, cut in cold butter until mixture is crumbly. Stir in cranberries and Gruyère. Gradually add 1½ cups cold buttermilk, stirring just until dry ingredients are moistened.

2 On a lightly floured surface, gently pat dough into a 10x8-inch rectangle. Fold dough into thirds, like a letter. Pat and fold dough two more times. Roll dough to 1-inch thickness. Using a 2½-inch round cutter, cut dough, rerolling scraps once. Place on prepared pan. Brush dough with remaining 2 tablespoons cold buttermilk. Sprinkle with sea salt, if desired.

3 Bake until golden brown, about 30 minutes. Let cool for 5 minutes on a wire rack; serve warm.

Apple Streusel Bread

*This sweetly spiced, cake-like bread has a generous
layer of apple in the middle that I can't resist.*

Bread:
- ½ cup unsalted butter, softened
- ⅓ cup plus 2 tablespoons firmly packed light brown sugar, divided
- ⅓ cup granulated sugar
- 2 large eggs, room temperature
- 1½ teaspoons vanilla extract
- 2 cups all-purpose flour
- 2 teaspoons baking powder
- ¼ teaspoon kosher salt
- ¾ cup whole milk, room temperature
- 3 cups chopped Gala apples (about 3 medium apples)
- ½ teaspoon ground cinnamon

Topping:
- ½ cup all-purpose flour
- 3 tablespoons firmly packed light brown sugar
- ½ teaspoon ground cinnamon
- 2 tablespoons unsalted butter, melted

Glaze:
- ½ cup confectioners' sugar
- 2 ounces cream cheese, softened
- 1 tablespoon whole milk

1 Preheat oven to 350°. Spray a 9x5-inch loaf pan with baking spray with flour.

2 **For bread:** In a large bowl, beat butter, ⅓ cup brown sugar, and granulated sugar with a mixer at medium speed until fluffy, 3 to 4 minutes, stopping to scrape sides of bowl. Add eggs, one at a time, beating well after each addition. Beat in vanilla.

3 In a medium bowl, whisk together flour, baking powder, and salt. With mixer on low speed, gradually add flour mixture to butter mixture alternately with milk, beginning and ending with flour mixture, beating just until combined after each addition.

4 In a medium bowl, toss together apples, cinnamon, and remaining 2 tablespoons brown sugar. Spread two-thirds of batter into prepared pan. Top with half of apple mixture. Spread remaining batter onto apples, and top with remaining apple mixture.

5 **For topping:** In a small bowl, whisk together flour, brown sugar, and cinnamon. Using a fork, stir in melted butter until crumbly. Sprinkle onto batter.

6 Bake until a wooden pick inserted in center comes out clean, 50 to 60 minutes. Let cool in pan for 15 minutes. Remove from pan, and let cool completely on a wire rack.

7 **For glaze:** In a medium bowl, beat confectioners' sugar and cream cheese with a mixer at medium-high speed until well combined. Beat in milk. Drizzle onto cooled bread. Store in an airtight container for up to 3 days.

Braided Honey Wheat Bread

MAKES 1 (12-INCH) ROUND LOAF

This beautiful plaited bread is truly a showstopper.

4 cups all-purpose
  flour
2 cups whole
  wheat flour
1 tablespoon salt
2 cups whole milk,
  warmed (105° to 110°)
¾ cup plus ⅓ cup
  honey, divided
1 tablespoon active
  dry yeast
½ cup unsalted
  butter, melted
2 large eggs, room
  temperature
½ cup unsalted
  butter, softened
1 large egg yolk
1 tablespoon water
Prepared whipped honey,
  to serve

1 In a large bowl, whisk together flours and salt. In another large bowl, stir together warm milk, ¾ cup honey, and yeast. Let stand until mixture is foamy, about 5 minutes. Add 1 cup flour mixture, melted butter, and eggs to yeast mixture, and beat with a mixer at medium speed until well combined. Gradually add remaining flour mixture, beating at low speed until a soft dough forms.

2 Turn out dough onto a heavily floured surface, and knead for 9 minutes, adding additional all-purpose flour as needed. (Dough will be slightly sticky.) Spray a large bowl with cooking spray. Place dough in bowl, turning to grease top. Cover with plastic wrap, and let rise in a warm, draft-free place (75°) until doubled in size, about 1 hour.

3 Line a large baking sheet with parchment paper. Spray the outside of a clean, empty 28-ounce can with cooking spray.

4 Punch down dough, and turn out onto a lightly floured surface. Roll dough into a 16x10-inch rectangle. In a small bowl, stir together softened butter and remaining ⅓ cup honey until well combined; spread mixture onto dough. Starting at one long side, roll up dough into a log, pinching seam to seal. Using a sharp knife, cut dough log in half lengthwise.

5 On prepared pan, carefully twist dough pieces around each other, cut side up, and shape into a circle around empty can. (Do not remove can.) Cover and let rise in a warm, draft-free place (75°) until doubled in size, about 45 minutes.

6 Preheat oven to 350°.

7 In a small bowl, whisk together egg yolk and 1 tablespoon water. Brush egg wash onto dough braid. Bake until golden brown and a wooden pick inserted near center comes out clean, 35 to 40 minutes. Let cool on pan for 10 minutes; remove can. Serve warm with whipped honey.

STEP-BY-STEP

STEP 1 Starting at one long side, roll dough rectangle into a log.

STEP 2 Using a sharp knife, cut dough log in half lengthwise.

STEP 3 With cut side of dough facing up, gently twist pieces around each other.

STEP 4 Shape dough into a circle around a clean, empty can to maintain its shape while it bakes.

Caramel Apple Spice Cake

I kick off apple season every year with this delicious spice cake. Paired with a rich caramel sauce, it takes traditional apple cake to the next level.

Cake:

- 1½ cups granulated sugar
- ¾ cup canola oil
- ¾ cup unsweetened applesauce
- ¾ cup prepared caramel sauce, plus more for serving
- 3 large eggs, room temperature
- 3¾ cups all-purpose flour
- 1 tablespoon baking powder
- 1½ teaspoons baking soda
- 1 teaspoon ground cinnamon
- ½ teaspoon kosher salt
- 1½ cups whole buttermilk, room temperature
- 2 medium Gala apples, peeled, cored, and finely chopped

Frosting:

- 1½ (8-ounce) packages cream cheese, softened
- ¾ cup unsalted butter, softened
- 6 cups confectioners' sugar
- 1 teaspoon vanilla extract

1 Preheat oven to 350°. Spray a 13x9-inch baking pan with baking spray with flour.

2 In the bowl of a stand mixer fitted with the whisk attachment, beat granulated sugar and oil at medium speed until well combined. Beat in applesauce and caramel. Add eggs, one at a time, beating well after each addition.

3 In a large bowl, whisk together flour, baking powder, baking soda, cinnamon, and salt. With mixer on low speed, gradually add flour mixture to sugar mixture alternately with buttermilk, beginning and ending with flour mixture, beating just until combined after each addition. Using a spatula, fold in apples, scraping bottom and sides of bowl. Spread batter in prepared pan.

4 Bake until cake springs back when lightly touched in center and a wooden pick inserted in center comes out clean, about 55 minutes. Let cool on a wire rack.

5 **For frosting:** In a large bowl, beat cream cheese and butter with a mixer at medium speed until smooth. Add confectioners' sugar, 1 cup at a time, beating well after each addition. Add vanilla, and beat at high speed for 1 minute. Spread frosting onto cake. Spoon desired amount caramel sauce onto frosting, and gently swirl into frosting using an offset spatula. Cover and refrigerate for up to 3 days.

Apple Cream Cheese Swirl Bundt Cake

MAKES 1 (15-CUP) BUNDT CAKE

I dare you not to fall in love with this beautiful cake. I sure have!

Filling:
- 1 (8-ounce) package cream cheese, softened
- ½ cup confectioners' sugar
- 2 tablespoons all-purpose flour
- 1 large egg, room temperature
- 1 teaspoon orange zest

Cake:
- 1½ cups unsalted butter, softened
- 1¾ cups firmly packed light brown sugar
- 4 large eggs, room temperature
- 3 large Granny Smith apples, peeled and cored
- 2 tablespoons fresh lemon juice
- 1 teaspoon orange zest
- 1 teaspoon vanilla extract
- 4 cups all-purpose flour
- 2 teaspoons ground cinnamon
- 1 teaspoon baking soda
- 1 teaspoon kosher salt
- ½ teaspoon ground ginger
- ⅛ teaspoon ground nutmeg

Glaze:
- 2 cups confectioners' sugar, sifted
- ¼ cup whole milk
- 3 tablespoons dark corn syrup

Garnish: chopped pecans

1 Preheat oven to 325°. Spray a 15-cup Bundt pan with baking spray with flour.

2 **For filling:** In a medium bowl, beat cream cheese with a mixer at medium speed until creamy. Add confectioners' sugar, flour, egg, and zest, and beat until smooth, about 2 minutes, stopping to scrape sides of bowl. Cover and refrigerate until ready to use.

3 **For cake:** In the bowl of a stand mixer fitted with the paddle attachment, beat butter and brown sugar at medium speed until fluffy, 3 to 4 minutes, stopping to scrape sides of bowl. Add eggs, one at a time, beating well after each addition.

4 Shred apples using the large holes of a box grater. Coarsely chop shredded apples. Add apples, lemon juice, zest, and vanilla to batter, and beat for 1 minute.

5 In a large bowl, whisk together flour, cinnamon, baking soda, salt, ginger, and nutmeg. With mixer on low speed, gradually add flour mixture to butter mixture, beating just until combined.

6 Spoon half of batter into prepared pan. Spoon filling onto batter, avoiding edges of pan. Top with remaining batter. Using a knife, pull blade back and forth through batter to swirl layers together. Smooth top of batter.

7 Bake until a wooden pick inserted near center comes out clean, about 1 hour and 15 minutes. Let cool in pan for 10 minutes. Remove from pan, and let cool completely on a wire rack.

8 **For glaze:** In a small bowl, whisk together confectioners' sugar, milk, and corn syrup until smooth. Drizzle glaze over cooled cake. Garnish with pecans, if desired. Cover and refrigerate for up to 3 days.

Butternut Squash Crumb Cake

Similar to ever-popular pumpkin, this squash variety is one of my favorites to bake with and tastes so sweet in this easy treat.

Topping:
- ¼ cup unsalted butter
- ⅓ cup firmly packed light brown sugar
- 1 teaspoon vanilla extract
- ¼ teaspoon kosher salt
- ¾ cup all-purpose flour
- 2 tablespoons confectioners' sugar
- ½ teaspoon pumpkin pie spice

Cake:
- 1 (1-pound) butternut squash, halved lengthwise and seeded
- 2 cups all-purpose flour
- 1 cup firmly packed light brown sugar
- 2 teaspoons baking powder
- ½ teaspoon baking soda
- 1½ teaspoons pumpkin pie spice
- ½ teaspoon kosher salt
- 3 large eggs, room temperature
- ¾ cup vegetable oil
- ½ cup sour cream
- 1 teaspoon vanilla extract

1 **For topping:** In a small saucepan, melt butter over medium heat. Whisk in brown sugar, vanilla, and salt until smooth. Remove from heat, and whisk in flour until smooth. Let cool completely. In a small bowl, whisk together confectioners' sugar and pie spice; cover and reserve.

2 Preheat oven to 350°. Line a large rimmed baking sheet with foil. Spray an 8-inch square baking pan with baking spray with flour.

3 **For cake:** Place squash, cut side down, on prepared baking sheet. Bake until tender, 30 to 40 minutes. Let stand until just cool enough to handle. Leave oven on.

4 Scoop squash pulp into the work bowl of a food processor; process until smooth. Transfer 1 cup puréed squash to a medium bowl; reserve remaining purée for another use.

5 In a large bowl, whisk together flour, brown sugar, baking powder, baking soda, pie spice, and salt. Whisk eggs, oil, sour cream, and vanilla into puréed squash. Add squash mixture to flour mixture, whisking just until smooth. Spread batter into prepared pan. Crumble topping onto batter.

6 Bake until a wooden pick inserted in center comes out clean, 40 to 45 minutes. Let cool completely in pan on a wire rack. Sift reserved confectioners' sugar mixture onto cake just before serving. Store in an airtight container for up to 3 days.

CHAPTER 7

Holiday Classics

I love Christmastime—all the sparkly decorations, catching up with friends, and, of course, baking for my loved ones. It fills my heart to see my family and friends enjoy the goodies I make for and with them. This chapter pays tribute to the holiday flavors that we all turn to year after year. I hope these recipes take you on a baking trip down memory lane and help you spread a little homemade Christmas cheer.

Holiday Fruitcake

This moist and flavorful version will change
everything you thought you knew about fruitcake.

2 (8-ounce) containers
  extra fancy fruit cake mix
1 (8-ounce) container
  candied red cherries,
  roughly chopped
1 cup golden raisins
⅓ cup brandy
1½ cups unsalted butter,
  softened
2 cups granulated sugar
6 large eggs, room
  temperature
1½ teaspoons vanilla extract
2¾ cups all-purpose flour
2 teaspoons baking powder
1½ teaspoons kosher salt
1½ teaspoons ground
  cinnamon
½ teaspoon ground allspice
½ teaspoon ground nutmeg
½ cup whole milk
1½ cups chopped pecans
Garnish: confectioners' sugar

1 In a medium bowl, combine fruit cake mix, cherries, raisins, and brandy. Let stand for 30 minutes.

2 Preheat oven 300°. Spray a 10-inch tube pan with baking spray with flour.

3 In a large bowl, beat butter and granulated sugar with a mixer at medium speed until fluffy, 3 to 4 minutes, stopping to scrape sides of bowl. Add eggs, one at a time, beating well after each addition. Beat in vanilla.

4 In a medium bowl, whisk together flour, baking powder, salt, cinnamon, allspice, and nutmeg. With mixer on low speed, gradually add flour mixture to butter mixture alternately with milk, beginning and ending with flour mixture, beating just until combined after each addition. Fold in fruit mixture and any remaining liquid in bowl and pecans. Spread batter into prepared pan.

5 Bake until a wooden pick inserted near center comes out clean, about 1 hour and 30 minutes. Let cool in pan for 15 minutes. Remove from pan, and let cool completely on a wire rack. Garnish with confectioners' sugar, if desired. Store in an airtight container for up to 5 days.

BAKING TIP

Cognac, bourbon, whiskey, or rum can be substituted for brandy. If you prefer
not to use alcohol, replace brandy with an equal amount of apple cider.

Gingerbread Layer Cake

From gingerbread houses to gingerbread cookies, this beloved flavor is a must for my family at Christmastime.

Cake:
- 2 cups unsulphured molasses
- 2 cups hot water
- 1 cup unsalted butter, softened
- 1 cup firmly packed dark brown sugar
- 2 large eggs, room temperature
- 2 teaspoons vanilla extract
- 5 cups all-purpose flour
- 2 tablespoons ground ginger
- 1 tablespoon baking powder
- 1 teaspoon ground allspice
- ¾ teaspoon kosher salt

Filling:
- 2 (8-ounce) containers mascarpone cheese, softened
- ¼ cup heavy whipping cream
- ¾ cup confectioners' sugar
- 1 teaspoon vanilla extract

Frosting:
- 1½ cups unsalted butter, softened
- ½ (8-ounce) package cream cheese, softened
- 5¾ cups confectioners' sugar
- ½ teaspoon ground ginger
- 3 tablespoons heavy whipping cream
- ½ teaspoon vanilla extract

Garnish: crumbled gingersnap cookies, chopped crystallized ginger

1 Preheat oven to 325°. Spray 2 (9-inch) round tall-sided cake pans with baking spray with flour.

2 For cake: In a medium bowl, stir together molasses and 2 cups hot water. Let cool for 10 to 15 minutes.

3 In a large bowl, beat butter and brown sugar with a mixer at medium speed until creamy, 3 to 4 minutes, stopping to scrape sides of bowl. Add eggs, one at a time, beating well after each addition. With mixer on low speed, beat in molasses mixture and vanilla.

4 In another large bowl, whisk together flour, ginger, baking powder, allspice, and salt. With mixer on low speed, gradually add flour mixture to butter mixture, beating until combined. Divide batter between prepared pans.

5 Bake until a wooden pick inserted in center comes out clean, 40 to 50 minutes. Let cool in pans for 10 minutes. Remove from pans, and let cool completely on wire racks.

6 For filling: In a medium bowl, beat mascarpone with a mixer at medium-low speed until creamy, about 1 minute. Gradually add cream, beating until just combined. Beat in confectioners' sugar and vanilla just until smooth.

7 For frosting: In a large bowl, beat butter and cream cheese with a mixer at medium speed until creamy, 2 to 3 minutes. Gradually add confectioners' sugar and ginger, beating until fluffy. Add cream and vanilla, and beat until a spreadable consistency is reached.

8 Spread mascarpone filling between layers. Spread frosting on top and sides of cake. Garnish with gingersnaps and ginger, if desired. Cover and refrigerate for up to 3 days.

White Chocolate Peppermint Poke Cake

MAKES 1 (13x9-INCH) CAKE

Everybody needs a festive poke cake in their
recipe box, and this one has a fun, minty twist.

1½ cups unsalted butter, softened

1¾ cups sugar

4 large egg whites, room temperature

2 large eggs, room temperature

3 teaspoons peppermint extract, divided

3½ cups all-purpose flour

1 tablespoon baking powder

½ teaspoon baking soda

½ teaspoon kosher salt

5 cups whole milk, divided

1 (4-ounce) bar white chocolate, melted

2 (3.4-ounce) boxes cheesecake instant pudding mix

1 (16-ounce) container frozen whipped topping, thawed

Garnish: crushed peppermint candies

1 Preheat oven to 350°. Spray a 13x9-inch baking dish with baking spray with flour.

2 In a large bowl, beat butter and sugar with a mixer at medium speed until fluffy, 3 to 4 minutes, stopping to scrape sides of bowl. Add egg whites and eggs, one at a time, beating well after each addition. Beat in 2 teaspoons extract.

3 In a medium bowl, whisk together flour, baking powder, baking soda, and salt. With mixer on low speed, gradually add flour mixture to butter mixture alternately with 1½ cups milk, beginning and ending with flour mixture, beating just until combined after each addition. Stir in melted chocolate. Spread batter into prepared pan.

4 Bake until a wooden pick inserted in center comes out clean, 45 to 55 minutes, covering with foil halfway through baking to prevent excess browning. Let cool in pan for 10 minutes. Using the handle of a wooden spoon, poke 1-inch-deep holes into warm cake at ½-inch intervals.

5 In a large bowl, whisk together pudding mixes, remaining 3½ cups milk, and remaining 1 teaspoon extract until thick and smooth. Slowly pour all over cake, spreading evenly with an offset spatula. Cover and refrigerate for at least 4 hours before serving or up to 3 days. Spread whipped topping onto cake just before serving. Garnish with peppermints, if desired.

BAKING TIP

To crush peppermint candies, place them in a heavy-duty resealable plastic bag, and firmly tap them with a rolling pin or meat mallet.

Hummingbird Cake

MAKES 1 (9-INCH) CAKE

Warm spices, sweet fruit, crunchy nuts, and creamy frosting—
this cake has everything you could want in a holiday dessert!

Cake:

- 3 cups all-purpose flour
- 2 cups granulated sugar
- 1 teaspoon baking soda
- 1 teaspoon kosher salt
- 1 teaspoon ground cinnamon
- 3 large eggs, room temperature
- 1½ cups vegetable oil
- 1 (8-ounce) can crushed pineapple, undrained
- 2 cups mashed ripe banana (about 5 medium bananas)
- 1 cup chopped pecans, toasted
- 1½ teaspoons vanilla extract

Frosting:

- ½ cup unsalted butter, softened
- 1 (8-ounce) package cream cheese, softened
- 1 (2-pound) package confectioners' sugar
- ¼ cup whole milk
- ⅛ teaspoon kosher salt
- 1 teaspoon vanilla extract

- 1½ cups chopped pecans, toasted

1 Preheat oven to 350°. Spray 2 (9-inch) round tall-sided cake pans with baking spray with flour.

2 For cake: In a large bowl, whisk together flour, granulated sugar, baking soda, salt, and cinnamon. In a medium bowl, whisk together eggs and oil. Stir egg mixture into flour mixture just until dry ingredients are moistened. Stir in pineapple, mashed banana, pecans, and vanilla until well combined. Divide batter between prepared pans.

3 Bake until a wooden pick inserted in center comes out clean, about 35 minutes. Let cool in pans for 10 minutes. Remove from pans, and let cool completely on wire racks.

4 For frosting: In a large bowl, beat butter and cream cheese with a mixer at medium speed until creamy. Gradually add confectioners' sugar, milk, and salt, beating until smooth and fluffy. Beat in vanilla.

5 Spread frosting between layers and on top and sides of cake. Press pecans onto bottom third of cake, and sprinkle on top of cake. Cover and refrigerate for up to 3 days.

Lemon-Gingerbread Trifle

The tart citrus and cranberry flavors in this lovely layered
dessert balance perfectly with the rich cake and fluffy filling.

Cake:
- 1 cup unsalted butter, softened
- 1½ cups sugar
- ¾ cup unsulphured molasses
- 4 large eggs, room temperature
- 3¼ cups all-purpose flour
- 2 teaspoons baking soda
- 2 teaspoons apple pie spice
- 1 teaspoon ground ginger
- ½ teaspoon kosher salt
- 1 cup sour cream, room temperature

Filling:
- 1 pound fresh or thawed frozen cranberries
- ⅔ cup maple syrup
- 3 cups cold heavy whipping cream
- 2 (10-ounce) jars lemon curd

Garnish: sugared rosemary sprigs

1 Preheat oven to 350°. Spray a 13x9-inch baking pan with baking spray with flour.

2 For cake: In a large bowl, beat butter and sugar with a mixer at medium speed until creamy, 3 to 4 minutes, stopping to scrape sides of bowl. Add molasses, beating until combined. Add eggs, one at a time, beating well after each addition.

3 In a medium bowl, whisk together flour, baking soda, pie spice, ginger, and salt. With mixer on low speed, gradually add flour mixture to butter mixture alternately with sour cream, beating just until combined. Spread batter into prepared pan.

4 Bake until a wooden pick inserted in center comes out clean, 30 to 35 minutes. Let cool completely in pan on a wire rack. Cut cake into 1½-inch cubes.

5 For filling: In a medium saucepan, bring cranberries and maple syrup to a boil over medium heat. Reduce heat, and simmer, stirring occasionally, until berries just begin to pop, about 10 minutes. Drain berries, discarding liquid; let cool completely.

6 In a large bowl, beat cream and lemon curd with a mixer at high speed until soft peaks form, stopping to scrape sides and bottom of bowl.

7 In a large trifle bowl, place one-third of cake cubes. Top with one-third of cream mixture and one-third of cranberries. Repeat layers twice. Cover and refrigerate for up to 1 day before serving. Garnish with sugared rosemary, if desired.

— **BAKING TIP** —

To make sugared rosemary, dredge lightly dampened rosemary sprigs in sugar until well coated. Let stand on a piece of parchment paper until dry, about 30 minutes.

German Chocolate Cake

Creamy chocolate frosting and fluffy layers pair
perfectly with the nutty texture of this festive cake.

Cake:
- 1 cup unsalted butter, softened
- 1 cup granulated sugar
- 1 cup firmly packed light brown sugar
- 4 large eggs, room temperature
- 2½ cups all-purpose flour
- ¼ cup unsweetened cocoa powder
- ½ teaspoon baking powder
- ½ teaspoon baking soda
- ½ teaspoon kosher salt
- 1½ cups whole buttermilk
- 6 ounces German's sweet baking chocolate, melted and cooled

Filling:
- 1½ cups granulated sugar
- 5 large egg yolks
- 1½ cups heavy whipping cream
- 6 tablespoons unsalted butter
- 2¼ cups sweetened flaked coconut
- 1½ cups toasted chopped pecans

Frosting:
- 1 cup unsalted butter, softened
- ¼ cup unsweetened cocoa powder
- ⅔ cup sour cream
- 5 cups confectioners' sugar
- 2 cups toasted chopped pecans

1 Preheat oven to 350°. Spray 2 (9-inch) round tall-sided cake pans with baking spray with flour.

2 For cake: In a large bowl, beat butter and sugars with a mixer at medium speed until fluffy, 3 to 4 minutes, stopping to scrape sides of bowl. Add eggs, one at a time, beating well after each addition.

3 In a medium bowl, whisk together flour, cocoa, baking powder, baking soda, and salt. With mixer on low speed, gradually add flour mixture to butter mixture alternately with buttermilk, beginning and ending with flour mixture, beating just until combined after each addition. Add melted chocolate, stirring until combined. Divide batter between prepared pans.

4 Bake until a wooden pick inserted in center comes out clean, 35 to 40 minutes. Let cool in pans for 10 minutes. Remove from pans, and let cool completely on wire racks.

5 For filling: In a medium saucepan, whisk together granulated sugar and egg yolks until combined; whisk in cream until smooth. Cook over medium heat, whisking frequently, until mixture is thick enough to coat the back of a spoon, 10 to 12 minutes. Remove from heat; stir in butter until melted. Stir in coconut and pecans until combined. Cover and refrigerate until filling is thick and cooled, at least 2 hours or up to 2 days.

6 For frosting: In a large bowl, beat butter and cocoa with a mixer at medium speed until creamy. Add sour cream, beating until smooth. Gradually add confectioners' sugar, beating until well combined.

7 Spread filling between layers. Spread frosting on top and sides of cake. Press pecans onto sides of cake. Cover and refrigerate for up to 3 days.

Red Velvet Crinkles

MAKES ABOUT 24

I keep my jars and tins filled all season long with
a double-batch of these soft and chewy cookies.

1 (15.25-ounce) box
   red velvet cake mix
⅓ cup vegetable oil
2 large eggs
2 tablespoons
   all-purpose flour
¼ teaspoon vanilla extract
1 cup granulated sugar
1 cup confectioners' sugar

1 In a large bowl, beat cake mix, oil, eggs, and flour with a mixer at medium speed for 2 minutes, stopping to scrape sides of bowl. Add vanilla, and beat until combined. Cover and refrigerate until firm, about 2 hours.

2 Preheat oven to 350°. Line baking sheets with parchment paper.

3 Place sugars in separate bowls. Scoop dough into 1½-inch balls. Roll in granulated sugar to coat; roll in confectioners' sugar to coat. Place 2 inches apart on prepared pans; slightly flatten cookies.

4 Bake until surface of cookies is cracked and edges look dry, 10 to 12 minutes. Let cool on pans for 5 minutes. Remove from pans, and let cool completely on wire racks. Store in an airtight container for up to 3 days.

Red Velvet Cupcakes

MAKES 28

The richness of these easy-to-make treats will have
you bringing them to all your Christmas celebrations.

Cupcakes:
- 1 cup unsalted butter, softened
- 2 cups granulated sugar
- 4 large eggs, room temperature
- 1 tablespoon vanilla extract
- 1 teaspoon apple cider vinegar
- 2½ cups all-purpose flour
- ⅓ cup unsweetened cocoa powder
- 1 teaspoon baking soda
- ½ teaspoon kosher salt
- 1 cup sour cream
- ½ cup whole milk
- 1 (1-ounce) bottle liquid red food coloring

Frosting:
- 1 cup unsalted butter, softened
- 1 (8-ounce) package cream cheese, softened
- 5 cups confectioners' sugar
- 1 tablespoon vanilla extract

Garnish: chopped pecans

1 Preheat oven to 350°. Line 28 muffin cups with foil or paper liners.

2 **For cupcakes:** In a large bowl, beat butter and granulated sugar with a mixer at medium speed until fluffy, 3 to 4 minutes, stopping to scrape sides of bowl. Add eggs, one at a time, beating well after each addition. Beat in vanilla and vinegar.

3 In a medium bowl, whisk together flour, cocoa, baking soda, and salt. In a small bowl, whisk together sour cream and milk. With mixer on low speed, gradually add flour mixture to butter mixture alternately with sour cream mixture, beginning and ending with flour mixture, beating just until combined after each addition. Stir in food coloring. Divide batter among prepared muffin cups, filling three-fourths full.

4 Bake until a wooden pick inserted in center comes out clean, 20 to 25 minutes. Let cool in pans for 10 minutes. Remove from pans, and let cool completely on wire racks.

5 **For frosting:** In a large bowl, beat butter and cream cheese with a mixer at medium speed until creamy, stopping to scrape sides of bowl. Gradually add confectioners' sugar, beating until smooth. Beat in vanilla. Spread or pipe frosting onto cupcakes. Garnish with pecans, if desired. Refrigerate in airtight containers for up to 3 days.

"I make these cupcakes especially for Michael. He adores red velvet cake."—Paula

Snowman Cupcakes

These cute creations are a great mix of craft and sweet treat, the perfect way for my grandbabies and me to spend time together in the kitchen.

1 (9-ounce) box yellow cake mix

½ cup cold water

1 large egg

⅛ teaspoon almond extract

¼ cup unsalted butter, softened

2 ounces cream cheese, softened

3½ cups confectioners' sugar, sifted

2 teaspoons heavy whipping cream

1 teaspoon vanilla extract

12 marshmallows

Colored piping gel

Fruit-flavored rolled candy sheets

1 Preheat oven to 350°. Line 12 muffin cups with foil liners.

2 In a large bowl, beat cake mix, ½ cup cold water, egg, and almond extract with a mixer at medium speed until thick and smooth, 3 to 4 minutes, stopping to scrape sides of bowl. Spoon batter into prepared muffin cups, filling halfway full.

3 Bake until a wooden pick inserted in center comes out clean, 15 to 20 minutes. Let cool completely.

4 In a large bowl, beat butter and cream cheese with a mixer at medium speed until creamy. Gradually add confectioners' sugar, beating until smooth. Beat in cream and vanilla until smooth.

5 Spread or pipe frosting onto cupcakes. Top each cupcake with a marshmallow. Use piping gel to add eyes, a nose, and a mouth to each marshmallow.

6 Cut fruit candy sheets into 12 (7x½-inch) strips. Wrap strips around base of marshmallows to form scarves. Let stand until frosting is set, about 15 minutes. Store in an airtight container for up to 2 days.

Eggnog Bundt Cake

This cake looks simple, but the tangy touch of
eggnog makes it a special Chrismas treat.

Cake:
- ¾ cup unsalted butter, softened
- 1¼ cups granulated sugar
- ¼ cup firmly packed light brown sugar
- 3 large eggs, room temperature
- 1½ teaspoons rum extract
- 3 cups all-purpose flour
- 1¾ teaspoons baking powder
- 1¼ teaspoons ground nutmeg
- 1 teaspoon kosher salt
- ½ teaspoon baking soda
- ½ teaspoon ground cinnamon
- ¾ cup prepared eggnog
- ½ cup whole milk

Glaze:
- 2 cups confectioners' sugar
- ¼ teaspoon rum extract
- 3 tablespoons whole milk

1 Preheat oven to 300°. Spray a 10-cup Bundt pan with baking spray with flour.

2 For cake: In a large bowl, beat butter and sugars with a mixer at medium speed until fluffy, 3 to 4 minutes, stopping to scrape sides of bowl. Add eggs, one at a time, beating well after each addition. Beat in rum extract.

3 In a medium bowl, whisk together flour, baking powder, nutmeg, salt, baking soda, and cinnamon. In a small bowl, stir together eggnog and milk. With mixer on low speed, gradually add flour mixture to butter mixture alternately with eggnog mixture, beginning and ending with flour mixture, beating just until combined after each addition. Spoon batter into prepared pan.

4 Bake until a wooden pick inserted near center comes out clean, 60 to 70 minutes. Let cool in pan for 15 minutes. Remove from pan, and let cool completely on a wire rack.

5 For glaze: In a medium bowl, whisk together confectioners' sugar and rum extract. Whisk in milk, 1 tablespoon at a time, until a thick, pourable consistency is reached. Drizzle glaze onto cooled cake. Store in an airtight container for up to 3 days.

New Japanese Fruitcake

This is my version of a spiced fruitcake that my grandmother and mama made when Bubba and I were growing up. When I started cooking our Christmas meal, I added the 7-minute frosting—it made a good thing even better!

Cake:
- 1 cup unsalted butter, softened
- 2 cups sugar
- 4 large eggs, room temperature
- 2 teaspoons vanilla extract
- 3 cups all-purpose flour
- 1 tablespoon baking powder
- 1 teaspoon kosher salt
- 1¼ cups whole milk
- 2 teaspoons pumpkin pie spice

Filling:
- 1 cup water
- 1 cup sugar
- 2 tablespoons cornstarch
- 1 (20-ounce) can crushed pineapple in juice, drained
- 1 cup sweetened flaked coconut
- Pinch kosher salt
- ⅔ cup dried tart cherries
- ⅓ cup minced crystallized ginger

Frosting:
- 2½ cups sugar
- 4 large egg whites, room temperature
- ½ cup water
- 2 tablespoons light corn syrup
- 2 teaspoons vanilla extract
- ½ teaspoon cream of tartar

1 Preheat oven to 350°. Spray 3 (9-inch) round cake pans with baking spray with flour. Line pans with parchment paper.

2 **For cake:** In a large bowl, beat butter and sugar with a mixer at medium speed until fluffy, 3 to 4 minutes, stopping to scrape sides of bowl. Add eggs, one at a time, beating well after each addition. Beat in vanilla.

3 In a medium bowl, whisk together flour, baking powder, and salt. With mixer on low speed, gradually add flour mixture to butter mixture alternately with milk, beginning and ending with flour mixture, beating just until combined after each addition.

4 Pour one-third of batter into a medium bowl; stir in pie spice. Spread spiced batter into one prepared pan. Divide remaining batter between remaining prepared pans.

5 Bake until a wooden pick inserted in center comes out clean, 15 to 20 minutes. Let cool in pans for 10 minutes. Remove from pans, and let cool completely on wire racks.

6 **For filling:** In a large saucepan, whisk together 1 cup water, sugar, and cornstarch until smooth. Stir in drained pineapple, coconut, and salt, and bring to a boil over medium heat. Cook, whisking constantly, until thickened, about 5 minutes. Remove from heat, and stir in cherries and ginger. Let cool completely.

7 Place one plain cake layer on a serving plate, and spread with half of filling. Top with spice cake layer, and spread with remaining filling. Top with remaining plain cake layer.

8 For frosting: In a medium saucepan, bring 1 inch of water to a simmer over medium heat. In the bowl of a stand mixer fitted with the whisk attachment, beat sugar, egg whites, ½ cup water, corn syrup, vanilla, and cream of tartar at low speed just until combined. Place bowl over pan of simmering water, and whisk by hand until sugar is dissolved and mixture is hot, about 3 minutes. Return bowl to stand mixer, and beat at high speed for 3 minutes. Continue beating until stiff peaks form, 5 to 7 minutes. Immediately spread frosting on top and sides of cake. Serve immediately.

Santa Hat Cookies

A baking sheet full of Christmas cookies is one of the many joys of the season, and my grandbabies have a blast piling these onto a plate for Santa!

Cookies:
- 1 (21-ounce) package sugar cookie mix
- ½ cup unsalted butter, melted
- 1 large egg
- 2 tablespoons all-purpose flour
- ½ teaspoon vanilla extract

Frosting:
- 1 cup unsalted butter, softened
- 4 cups confectioners' sugar, sifted
- 2 tablespoons heavy whipping cream
- ¼ teaspoon orange extract
- Red paste food coloring

White sanding sugar
Miniature marshmallows

1 For cookies: In a large bowl, stir together cookie mix, melted butter, egg, flour, and vanilla until a soft dough forms. Cover and refrigerate for 1 hour.

2 Preheat oven to 350°. Line baking sheets with parchment paper.

3 On a lightly floured surface, roll dough to ¼-inch thickness. Using a 2-inch triangle-shaped cutter, cut dough, gently rerolling scraps to use all dough. Place 2 inches apart on prepared pans.

4 Bake until edges are golden brown, 9 to 11 minutes. Let cool on pans for 5 minutes. Remove from pans, and let cool completely on wire racks.

5 For frosting: In a large bowl, beat butter with a mixer at medium speed until creamy. Gradually add confectioners' sugar, beating until smooth. Add cream and orange extract, beating until well combined.

6 Spoon one-third of frosting into a pastry bag fitted with a medium round tip. Tint remaining frosting with red food coloring as desired. Spread red frosting onto cookies, leaving a ½-inch border at bottom of triangle. Pipe white frosting onto area at base of triangles, and sprinkle with sanding sugar. Pipe a dot of white frosting at top of triangle, and top with a marshmallow. Let stand until frosting is dry. Store in an airtight container for up to 3 days.

Black Forest Cake

The combination of sweet cherries and
devil's food cake in this dessert is just divine.

1 (15.25-ounce) box devil's
food chocolate cake mix
1¼ cups water, divided
⅓ cup vegetable oil
3 large eggs
¼ cup granulated sugar
¾ teaspoon cherry
extract, divided
2 cups cold heavy
whipping cream
¾ cup confectioners' sugar
1 cup frozen dark sweet
cherries, thawed, halved,
patted dry, and divided
Garnish: grated chocolate,
chocolate curls

1 Preheat oven to 350°. Spray 2 (8-inch) round cake pans with
cooking spray. Line bottom of pans with parchment paper.

2 In a large bowl, beat cake mix, 1 cup water, oil, and eggs with
a mixer at low speed just until combined. Increase mixer speed to
medium, and beat for 2 minutes. Divide batter between prepared pans.

3 Bake until a wooden pick inserted in center comes out clean, about
26 minutes. Let cool in pans for 10 minutes. Remove from pans, and
let cool completely on a wire rack.

4 In a small saucepan, bring granulated sugar and remaining ¼ cup
water to a boil over medium-high heat; cook for 3 minutes. Remove
from heat; let cool to lukewarm. Add ½ teaspoon cherry extract;
stir well. Using a fork, poke holes in top of cake layers. Slowly spoon
sugar mixture all over layers until absorbed. Let stand for 10 minutes.

5 In a large chilled bowl, beat cream with a mixer at medium-high
speed until slightly thickened. Gradually add confectioners' sugar,
beating until stiff peaks form. Add remaining ¼ teaspoon cherry
extract, beating until combined.

6 Place one cake layer on a cake plate. Spread with one-third of
whipped cream, and top with ¾ cup cherries. Top with remaining
cake layer. Spread remaining whipped cream on top and sides of
cake, and top with remaining ¼ cup cherries. Garnish with grated
chocolate and chocolate curls, if desired. Refrigerate for at least
3 hours before serving or up to overnight.

BAKING TIP

To make chocolate curls, microwave chocolate block on high in 15-second intervals until
chocolate is slightly warm. Use a vegetable peeler to shave thin strips of chocolate into curls;
freeze in an airtight container until ready to use. Use a rasp-style zester to finely grate chocolate.

Recipe Index

Recipe Index

Photography Credits

Matt Armendariz: pages 2, 64, 86, 108, 122, 139, 173, 182, 186, 224, 239, 256

Kelli Boyd: front cover, pages 6, 10, 12, 21, 54, 144, 164, 233

Deborah Whitlaw Llewellyn: pages 109 (hands), 153, 187 (hands), 203, 207, 225 (hands), 255

Product Resources

Cover: Savannah Trellis plates
Page 49: Country Barnyard mug
Page 73: Vineyard Basket bowls
Page 89: Garden Rooster tool
    crock and bowls
Page 121: Vineyard Basket plate
Page 144: Country Barnyard
    spatula
Page 164: Indigo Blossom mug
Page 167: Indigo Blossom plates
Page 168: Garden Rooster bowl
Page 204: Vineyard Basket mugs

Products are available through
pauladeenshop.com and at Paula Deen
retail stores. Visit *pauladeen.com/stores*
for more information.

Acknowledgments

This book would not be possible without the love, support, and hard work of so many people. First, I want to thank my family. You provide the reason and the inspiration for everything that I do. I'm so blessed with my co-captain through life, my husband, Michael.

My sons, Jamie and Bobby, have helped me become the person I am today, and I am so grateful for their unconditional love. It's such a joy to watch Jamie, his wife, Brooke, and their children, Jack and Matthew; Bobby, his wife, Claudia, and their children, Olivia, Amelia, and Linton; my stepdaughter, Michelle, her husband, Daniel, and their children, Henry and John; my stepson, Anthony, his wife, Ashley, and their son, Bennett; and my niece, Corrie, her husband, Brian, and their son, Sullivan, carry on the traditions of our family.

Thank you to my brother, Bubba, and to my Aunt Peggy. You are my links to our past generations, and you never let me forget where I come from. And thank you to my best friend, Susan "Bubbles" Greene, for always being there.

I want to thank everyone at Hoffman Media, the company that publishes my magazine, *Cooking with Paula Deen*. Its founder and president, Phyllis Hoffman DePiano, is a brilliant businesswoman and, more importantly, my dear friend. Phyllis and her sons, Brian Hart Hoffman and Eric Hoffman, proposed the idea for this book to me a year ago. With my love of baking and their talent at publishing, it was a no-brainer for me. Their team has truly helped make this something to be so proud of. Thank you to Greg Baugh and Brooke Bell for guiding this book from start to finish and to Nancy Meeks for managing it daily.

Of course, books are nothing without the talented team of people to bring a vision to life, so I thank these folks wholeheartedly: art director Cailyn Haynes; editors Whitney Durrwachter, Fran Jensen, and Meg Lundberg; writers Katherine Cloninger and Daniel Dubuisson; recipe developers and food stylists Vanessa Rocchio, Irene Yeh, Ashley Jones, Jade Sinacori, Erin Mehar, Theresa Kelley, Sally Pickle, and Meta Adler; prop stylists Lucy Finney, Caroline Blum, and Mary Beth Jones; photographers William Dickey, Stephanie Welbourne Steele, Nicole Du Bois, Matt Armendariz, Kelli Boyd, and Deborah Whitlaw Llewellyn; and image specialists Delisa McDaniel and Clark Densmore. Thank you to Tricia Williams for your marketing expertise.

Thanks to the folks who work here at our home: Patrick and Amanda Dobbs and Mike Styer. They all allow me to be free to do what I do. To our team who mans our Savannah office: Theresa Feuger, Cassie Powers, Melinda Rushing, Stephanie Peay, and Kinzie Collett, thank y'all so much.

It goes without saying how thankful I am for the staff at The Lady and Sons and Paula Deen's Creek House in Savannah, and Paula Deen's Family Kitchen in Pigeon Forge, Tennessee; Myrtle Beach, South Carolina; San Antonio, Texas; Fairview, Texas; Panama City Beach, Florida; Destin, Florida; Branson, Missouri; and Foley, Alabama. They all bring the same hospitality, love, and attention to my recipes there as I do in my home kitchen. Others who are so close to my heart are those on my team in Buffalo, New York, headed by Paula Deen Ventures President Steve Nanula, Nick Gallegos, Anthony Nanula, and Debbie Lanoye. Emily Warren Peterson, thank you for keeping me looking my best.

I'm sending a big hug to my business partner and CEO, Bob McManus, to Kaiser Swann, and to their team in Tennessee.

I send out so much love to Eddie Zorawowicz, the most incredible assistant, whom most folks only dream of having. He brings calm to chaos.

Last but certainly not least, to all my fans: Your support means the world to me, and it is because of all of you that I still have the good fortune to be doing what I love, bringing loved ones from all over together around the table.